W9-CFM-406

Acknowledgements

We would like to thank the following individuals for their comments and suggestions on earlier versions of this book:

Keith Adams
Kevin Bergman
Charles M. Browne
Kaori Kato
Leslie Koustaff
Lynn Mitchell
Rosemary Reynolds
Joseph Tomei

This book would not have been possible without the students and staff at the ELS Center in San Francisco, Miyagi Gakuin, Temple University, and Language Institute of Japan. We appreciate their ideas and assistance in developing this project.

We wish to acknowledge all of our professional colleagues who influenced us in shaping this book and the accompanying teaching notes. In particular, we wish to thank Mario Rinvolucri and Penny Ur for their work which has encouraged us to look for ways to breathe new life, communication, and interest into activities.

We would also like to thank all the people in the Longman Group and Lingual House team who advised on and supported this work, especially Damien Tunnacliffe, Helena Gomm, Dugie Cameron, Shinsuke Suzuki, Hiromi Tsuchiya, Hideki Komiyama, Tadashi Hata, Kevin Bergman, Sean Kao, Jill Wang, and Jung-ja Lee. In particular, we'd like to thank our editor, Mike Rost, our project coordinator, Keiko Kimura and our designer, Valerie Randall, for their direction and insights.

Finally, we would like to thank June Komater and Nathan McClure, Cathy Hendrix and Karl Murphy, and Masumi and Kent Helgesen for their personal support.

mh km ap

Contents

Marc Helgesen

Kevin McClure

Amy Parker

Talking Together

LINGUAL HOUSE

Published by
Longman Asia ELT
A division of Longman Asia Ltd
18th Floor, cornwall House
Taikoo Place
979 King's Road
Hong Kong
Tel: (852) 811 8168

and Associated Companies throughout the world

© Longman Asia Limited 1993

*This book was developed for Longman Asia ELT by Lateral Communications Ltd.
Lingual House is an imprint of Longman Asia ELT.*

First published 1993
Reprinted 1995

Produced by Longman Asia Limited
Printed in China
SWT/04

ISBN 0 582 10240 5

The
publisher's
policy is to use
**paper manufactured
from sustainable forests**

Introduction

Our students are ready to speak in English — and they have a lot to say. Often, however, beginning–level students have difficulty with oral English classes. Although our students may have studied English in the past, they often have not had the *support* or *motivation* to use English to communicate.

Talking Together is designed to provide both that support and the motivation. This book is a first speaking course for students of English as a foreign or second language. Its *task-based syllabus* and *step–by–step progression* make it effective with students who, although they may have previously studied English, have had little experience with the spoken language.

The careful progression of each unit ensures that students receive ample practice and support in speaking. All students will be able to accomplish the tasks that are presented. The first two pages of each unit of *Talking Together* consist of about four preparation activities of the following types: Pronunciation, Choice, Focus, Conversation Guide, and Group Response.

Pronunciation
Talking Together includes two types of Pronunciation Exercises. In some units, the emphasis is on the stress and timing of phrases and syllables. In other units, the emphasis is on the pronunciation of vocabulary used in the unit. In this section, the students hear clear models and attempt to repeat the model pronunciation.

Choice
These are activities where two answers are given. Students listen and decide which is correct. The procedure is similar to that for the Pronunciation Exercises.

Focus
Focus activities are exercises in which the students listen for and write specific information. They utilize the vocabulary that the students will need in the upcoming interactive practices.

Conversation Guide
These are dialogues which present useful models of conversation and interaction. These conversation guides prepare the students directly for the kind of interaction they will do in the pair practice section.

Group Response
The Group Response activities are oral drills which require decision-making. These exercises build familiarity and confidence so each student is able to move on to more open situations.

The order of these exercises varies, depending on the language point being presented. The activities prepare students for the more intensive and personal communication that takes place during the Pair Practice which follows. They do this by introducing the topic and familiarizing the students with the vocabulary and sentence patterns the students will use. All of the preparation activities are included on the cassette tapes that accompany *Talking Together*. Specific procedures and teaching suggestions for each section can be found in the Classroom Notes which begin on page 75.

Pair Practice

The third and fourth pages of each unit are Pair Practice. These practices provide motivating, intensive exercises for each student, which allow the students to develop both fluency and accuracy in spoken English.

Just as teacher–led instruction is valuable for learning a language, pair practice is recognized as an effective and important part of learning language. Pair practice provides a far greater *quantity of oral practice —* certainly an essential part of any English class. Finding ways to increase the quantity of practice is especially important in the large classes that many teachers face. These activities also provide *quality practice*. In information exchanges, students communicate with a purpose — this ensures that they understand what they are saying and that they will try to understand their partners.

In these exercises, students work in pairs, without the teacher to tell them what to say. In each pair, one student is "A", the other "B". The A student looks only at the A page, while the B student looks only at the B page. Since the activities involve clear outcomes and results, they provide excellent feedback to you as teacher. You will know who has accomplished the goal and who still needs more work. Teaching procedures and additional suggestions (including how to deal with problems that can arise with students unfamiliar with this type of learning) are included in the Classroom Notes at the end of this book.

Review Units

Units 5, 10 and 15 are followed by a one page Social Conversation section. This page consists of a Conversation Guide and a Group Response focusing on different types of interaction such as greeting, responding, and apologizing. It is followed by a review lesson, "The Small Talk Game." This game, played in groups of four, recycles the language points of the previous five units.

Talking Together does more than allow students to learn and practice English. It recognizes that our students can *interact* in English. It provides the support and motivation for them to do so.

Pronunciation

Listen. Repeat.

What's your name?   My name's <u>Mari</u>.

I'm <u>Mari</u>.

Where do you live?   In <u>Osaka</u>.

What do you do?   I'm a student.

What do you do in your free time?   I listen to music. I like jazz.

FOCUS

HINT ☞	**If you don't understand, ask.**	Could you repeat that?
		What does .... mean?
		How do you spell that?

Ask questions about this woman. Listen. Write the answers.

1. What's her name? *Her name's* ....

2. Where does she live? ....

3. What does she do? ....

4. What does she do in her free time? ....

Listen. Write the information.

1. What's his name? ....

2. Where does he live? ....

3. What does he do? ....

4. What does he do in his free time? ....

CONVERSATION GUIDE

Listen.

1. A: Where does Ms. Lima live?   B: Excuse me?
   A: Where does she live?   B: In San Francisco.

2. A: What does Mr. Williams do?   B: He's a teacher.
   A: What does he do in his free time? B: He likes watching movies.

Practice the conversations.

GroupRESPONSE

Look at the chart. Listen and answer the questions.

NAME	Ms. Lima	Mr. Williams	Mr. Choy	Ms. Ito
LIVES IN	San Francisco	New York	Seoul	Honolulu
JOB	Lawyer	Teacher	Student	Taxi Driver
INTERESTS	Driving	Watching movies	Listening to music	Hiking

Now listen again and check your answers.

You are A

What does Larry do?

Your partner is B

He's retired.

NAME		LIVES IN	OCCUPATION	FREE TIME ACTIVITY
Jim			pilot	
Mia		Atlanta		dancing
Rita			student	
Larry		Toronto		camping

1. Look at the chart. Ask B these questions. Write the information on the chart.

Where does Jim live?   Where does Rita live?

What does he like to do?   What does she do in her free time?

What does Mia do?   What does Larry do?

HINT 👉   **Be sure you understand:**   Excuse me? Could you repeat that?
What does .... mean?
How do you spell that?

2. Answer B's questions.

3. Ask B the questions. Write the answers on the chart.

Personal Information Sheet

1. Name ....
   WHAT'S YOUR NAME?

2. Lives ....
   WHERE DO YOU LIVE?

3. Job ....
   WHAT DO YOU DO?

4. Free time activity ....
   WHAT DO YOU DO IN YOUR FREE TIME?

5. Music ....
   WHAT KIND OF MUSIC DO YOU LIKE?

4. Answer B's questions.

JUST
FOR
FUN

Close your book. What can you remember about B? Say the things. B will say, "That's right." or "That's wrong." Now tell five more things about yourself.

For example:
My favorite sport is... My favorite artist is... My favorite color is... Can B remember all five?

Your partner is A	You are B

What does Jim do?

He's a pilot.

NAME	LIVES IN	OCCUPATION	FREE TIME ACTIVITY
Jim	Miami		hiking
Mia		designer	
Rita	Rio de Janeiro		swimming
Larry		retired (STOPPED WORKING)	

1. Look at the chart. Answer A's questions.

2. Ask A these questions. Write the information on the chart.

What does Jim do?

What does Rita do?

Where does Mia live?

Where does Larry live ?

What does she like to do?

What does he do in his free time?

HINT 	Be sure you understand:	Excuse me? Could you repeat that? What does .... mean? How do you spell that?

3. Answer A's questions about yourself.

4. Ask A the questions. Write the answers on the chart.

Personal Information Sheet

1. Name ....
   WHAT'S YOUR NAME?

2. Lives ....
   WHERE DO YOU LIVE?

3. Job ....
   WHAT DO YOU DO?

4. Free time activity ....
   WHAT DO YOU DO IN YOUR FREE TIME?

5. Music ....
   WHAT KIND OF MUSIC DO YOU LIKE?

JUST FOR FUN

Close your book. What can you remember about A? Say the things. A will say, "That's right." or "That's wrong."

Now tell five more things about yourself. Can A remember all five?

FOCUS

Listen. Write the numbers.

HINT	Be sure you understand:	Could you repeat that? What does .... mean?

a.	f. .... students	k. .... men and .... women
b.	g. .... teachers	l. .... books and .... magazines
c.	h. .... people	m. .... students and .... teachers
d.	i. .... Americans	n. .... buildings and .... rooms
e.	j. .... children	o. .... Japanese, ... Koreans, and .... Chinese

Pronunciation

Listen.

HINT	Some parts of the words (syllables) are longer. **long=____ short=__**

a. (13) thirteen	(30) thirty	f. (22) twenty-two
b. (14) fourteen	(40) forty	g. (47) forty-seven
c. (16) sixteen	(60) sixty	h. (66) sixty-six
d. (17) seventeen	(70) seventy	i. (79) seventy-nine
e. (19) nineteen	(90) ninety	j. (86) eighty-six
		k. (91) ninety-one

Now listen and say the numbers.

CHOICE

Circle the number you hear.

a.	15	50	b.	19	90	c.	14	40	d.	17	70
e.	13	30	f.	12	20	g.	80	88	h.	50	55
i.	16	69	j.	37	73						

CONVERSATION GUIDE

Listen.

1. A: How many tickets do you have?   B: I have FIFTEEN.
   A: What did you say?   B: FIFTEEN.
   A: Thanks.

2. A: How many students are in your class?   B: There are FIFty.
   A: Did you say 'FIFTEEN' or 'FIFty'?   B: I said, 'FIFty.'
   A: Fifty? Thanks.

Practice the conversations.

You are A   **Your partner is B**

How many cans
of soda do we need?   Twelve.

1. You're planning a party. Ask B.   Write the answer.

a. How many (pizzas)   do we have?   ....

b. How many (music videos) do we have?   ....

c. How many 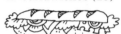 (cans of soda) do we need?   ....

d. How many (people)   are coming?   ....

2. Answer B.

e. Glasses (30)   f. CD's (14)   g. Plates (50)   h. Sandwiches (15)

3. Ask B.

i. How many (flowers)   does (Tomo) have? ....

j. How many (TVs)   does   have? ....

k. How many (video tapes) does   have? ....

l. How many (dogs)   does   have? ....

4. Answer B.

JUST FOR FUN

How many? Ask your partner: How many .... do you have now?

keys   pens and pencils   books   buttons   coins

Add five more things.

PAGE B

Pair Practice

Your partner is A   **You are B**

How many cans of soda do we need?   Twelve.

1. You're planning a party. Answer A.

a. Pizzas (5)   b. Music Videos (14)   c. Cans of soda (12)   d. People (25)

   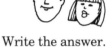

2. Ask A.   Write the answer.

e. How many (glasses)   do we have?   ....

f. How many (CD's)   should I bring?   ....

g. How many (plates)   do we need?   ....

h. How many (sandwiches) should we make?   ....

3. Answer A.

4. Ask A.

l. How many  (cats)   does (Marta) have?   ....

m. How many (computers) does   have?   ....

o. How many (posters)   does   have?   ....

p. How many (books)   does   have?   ....

JUST FOR FUN

How many? Ask your partner: How many .... do you have now?

keys   pens and pencils   books   buttons   coins

Add five more things.

Pronunciation

Look at the clocks. Listen. Repeat the times.

1:00
It's one o'clock

1:15
It's one-fifteen (or)
It's a quarter past one

1:30
It's one-thirty (or)
It's half past one

1:45
It's one-forty-five (or)
It's a quarter to two

1:10
It's one-ten (or)
It's ten past one

1:20
It's one-twenty (or)
It's twenty past one

1:40
It's one-forty (or)
It's twenty to two

1:50
It's one-fifty (or)
It's ten to two

12:00
It's twelve o'clock
☼ It's noon
☾ It's midnight

GroupRESPONSE

Look at the bus schedule. Listen to the questions. Say the answers.
Note: The northbound bus leaves San Diego at 5:30. Then it goes to Los Angeles. It leaves Los Angeles at 8:59. Then it goes to Santa Barbara, etc.

Bus Schedule

San Diego to San Francisco	(northbound)	Arrival Times	Departure Times
San Diego		—	5:30 A.M.
Los Angeles		8:41 A.M.	8:59 A.M.
Santa Barbara		10:44 A.M.	10:59 A.M.
Monterey		3:14 P.M.	3:30 P.M.
San Francisco		7:00 P.M.	—

San Francisco to San Diego	(southbound)	Arrival Times	Departure Times
San Francisco		—	7:00 A.M.
Monterey		11:38 A.M.	12 NOON
Santa Barbara		3:25 P.M.	3:30 P.M.
Los Angeles		6:23 P.M.	6:45 P.M.
San Diego		9:30 P.M.	—

Now listen again and check your answers.

CONVERSATION GUIDE

Listen.

1. A: Excuse me. What time is it?   B: It's two o'clock.
   A: Thanks.   B: You're welcome.

2. A: Is it three o'clock yet?   B: No, it isn't. It's two forty-five.
   A: OK. Thanks.   B: You're welcome.

Practice the conversations.

FOCUS

Listen. Write the times.

a. _____ : _____   f. _____ : _____

b. _____ : _____   g. _____ : _____

c. _____ : _____   h. _____ : _____

d. _____ : _____   i. _____ : _____

e. _____ : _____   j. _____ : _____

You are A | **Your partner is B**

What time does
Carl get up?

At 6:45.

1. Answer B's questions.

Carl

6:45   7:10   7:38   8:00   11:30   1:20   3:50   6:00   8:30   11:00

2. What time does Emi do these things?
Ask B the times. Draw the hands on the clocks.

Emi

get up | eat breakfast | catch the train | arrive at work | eat lunch | have a meeting | go home | cook dinner | watch TV | go to bed

3. Show these times with two pencils on a desk. B will guess them.

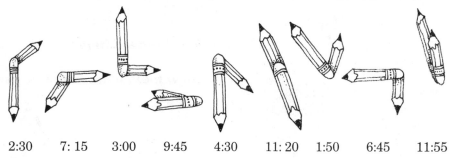

2:30   7: 15   3:00   9:45   4:30   11: 20   1:50   6:45   11:55

4. B will show different times with two pencils. Guess them.

JUST
FOR
FUN

Quickly write a list of your daily activities.
Tell B about your schedule.
Find at least five things you both do at the same time.
Circle them.
Find five things you do at different times.
Underline them.

PAGE B

Pair Practice

Your partner is A **You are B**

1. What time does Carl do these things?
Ask A the times. Draw the hands on the clocks.

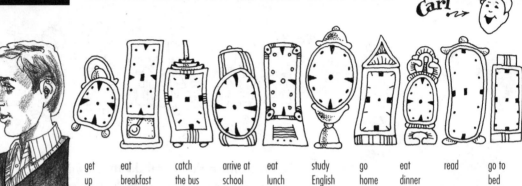

Carl

| get up | eat breakfast | catch the bus | arrive at school | eat lunch | study English | go home | eat dinner | read | go to bed |

What time does
Emi go to bed?

At 11:30.

2. Answer A's questions.

Emi

7:00   7:30   8:14   8:50   12:40   1:45   5:00   6:30   8:00   11:30

3. A will show different times with two pencils. Guess them.

4. Show these times with two pencils on a desk. A will guess them.

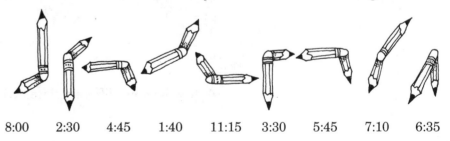

8:00   2:30   4:45   1:40   11:15   3:30   5:45   7:10   6:35

JUST FOR FUN

Quickly write a list of your daily activities.
Tell A about your schedule.
Find at least five things you both do at the same time.
Circle them.
Find five things you do at different times.
Underline them.

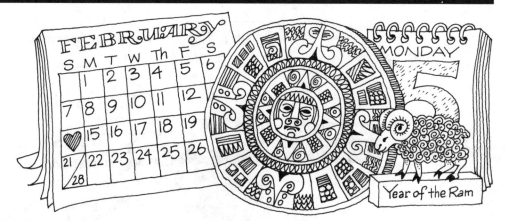

Year of the Ram

FOCUS

Listen. Write only the dates. Don't write the sentences.

1. ....   6. ....

2. ....   7. ....

3. ....   8. ....

4. ....   9. ....

5. ....   10. ....

Spelling Check: **Months**	1. January	5. May	9. September
	2. February	6. June	10. October
	3. March	7. July	11. November
	4. April	8. August	12. December

HINT 👉

| Months and years: | Use **in** |
| Days and dates: | Use **on** |

CHOICE

Listen. Repeat the sentences. Circle on or in.

1. New Year's is on / in January.

2. Ms. Park's birthday is on / in July.

3. Janet was born on / in December 10, 1972.

4. School begins on Monday and finishes on / in Friday.

5. They went to Taiwan on / in 1991.

6. I graduated from university on / in June, 1990.

CONVERSATION GUIDE

HINT 👉 For dates, say the numbers like this:

1 = first	(1st, 21st, 31st)
2 = second	(2nd, 22nd)
3 = third	(3rd, 23rd)
other numbers	= + th (fourth, fifth, eleventh, thirteenth...)

Listen.

1. A: Pardon me.
   What's the date today?   B: It's Monday, the 18th.
   A: The 18th?   B: Yes.

2. A: Excuse me.
   When's the science test?   B: It's on the 23rd.
   A: The 23rd?   B: That's right.

3. A: Pardon me. When were
   the Barcelona Olympics?   B: They were in 1992.
   A: 1992? Thanks.   B: Sure.

Practice the conversations.

GroupRESPONSE

Look at the calendar. Listen to the questions. Say the answers.

JULY		1	2	3 Barbecue 7:30	4 Independence Day	5 Baseball Game
6	7 Economics Test	8 12:00–1:30 Lunch with Tom	9	10 Last day of CLASS!	11 Concert	12 VACATION STARTS →
13 →	14 →	15 →	16 →	17 →	18 →	19 →
20 →	21 BACK TO WORK ☹	22	23	24	25	26
27	28	29 Anne's Birthday	30	31		

Now listen again and check your answers.

 You are A   **Your partner is B**

1. Ask B. Write the information on the calendar.
When's the next English test? ...the soccer game? ...Emi's party?

Sun	Mon	Tues	Wed	Thurs	Fri	Sat
	1	2	3	4	5	6
7	8 *Piano Concert*	9	10 *Math Test*	11	12 *Lee's Birthday*	13

When is
Emi's party?   It's on ....

2. Answer B's questions.

3. Ask B. Write the answers.

1. Did Columbus visit America in 1490 or 1492?   ....
2. Was the Beatles' last concert in 1969 or 1971?   ....
3. Did Bell invent the telephone in 1876 or 1986?   ....
4. Did Shakespeare die in 1660 or 1616?   ....

Event	Year
Marco Polo visited China:	1271
Mona Lisa painted:	1505
President Kennedy died:	1963
Apollo 9 reached the moon:	1969

4. Answer B's question. It was in .... (year).

5. When?
This is a guessing game. Read your questions (*) to your partner.
Your partner will answer. Is your partner correct? Listen to your partner's
questions. Guess the answers. Were you correct?

* 1.   When were the Seoul Olympics? (1988)
  2.   ☐ 1927   ☐ 1930   ☐ 1935
* 3.   When did the first McDonald's in Russia open? (1990)
  4.   ☐ January   ☐ October   ☐ November
* 5.   When did World War One start? (1914)
  6.   ☐ 1985   ☐ 1988   ☐ 1991
* 7.   When is Thanksgiving Day in Canada? (October)
  8.   ☐ Thursday   ☐ Friday   ☐ Monday
* 9.   When did Elvis Presley die? (1977)
  10. ☐ 1969   ☐ 1979   ☐ 1989

Your score : ..../ 5   Your partner's score: ..../ 5

 JUST FOR FUN   Think of 5 more famous dates that you know.
Write them down. Ask your partner: "What
happened on / in .... ?"
How many can your partner guess?

| Your partner is A | You are B |

When is
Emi's party?   It's on ....

Event	Year
Columbus visited America:	1492
Beatles' last concert:	1969
Bell invented telephone:	1876
Shakespeare died:	1616

1. Answer A's questions.

Sun	Mon 1	Tues 2	Wed 3	Thurs 4 English Test	Fri 5	Sat 6 Emi's Party
7	8	9	10	11	12	13 Soccer Game 2 pm.

2. Ask A. Write the information on the calendar.
When's Lee's birthday? ... the math test? ... the piano concert?

3. Answer A's questions. It was in .... (year).

4. Ask A. Write the answers.

1. Did Marco Polo go to China in 1271 or 1317?   ....

2. Was the Mona Lisa finished in 1505 or 1605?   ....

3. Was President Kennedy killed in 1960 or 1963?   ....

4. Did people first go to the moon in 1968 or 1969?   ....

5. When?
This is a guessing game. Read your questions (*). Guess the answers.
Check (✓) the correct answers. Are A's answers correct?

   1.   ☐ 1984   ☐ 1986   ☐ 1988

* 2.   When did Disney first draw Mickey Mouse? (1927)

   3.   ☐ 1919   ☐ 1990   ☐ 1993

* 4.   When are most U.S. elections held? (November)

   5.   ☐ 1914   ☐ 1917   ☐ 1940

* 6.   When did Korea join the United Nations? (1991)

   7.   ☐ October   ☐ November   ☐ December

* 8.   What day is the U.S. Thanksgiving holiday? (Thursday)

   9.   ☐ 1967   ☐ 1973   ☐ 1977

*10.   When did Michael Jackson make his first hit record? (1969)

Your score : ········ / 5   Your partner's score: ········ / 5

JUST
FOR
FUN

Think of 5 more famous dates that you know.
Write them down. Ask your partner: "What
happened on / in .... ?"
How many can your partner guess?

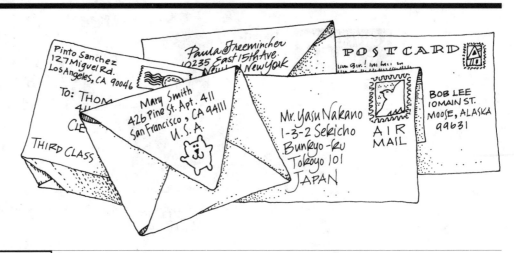

A Typical U.S. Address:

Mary Smith	*person's name*
426 Pine St.	*street address*
Apt. 411	*apartment number*
San Francisco, CA	*city and state*
94111	*zip (postal) code*

**Group**RESPONSE

Put the addresses in order. Number the lines.
Say the addresses.

....	33610	....	San Diego, California
....	8619 N. 14th Ave.	....	Mr. Y. S. Kim
....**1**......	Ms. Maria Moss	....	92101
....	Tampa, Florida	....	89135 N. Pacific Blvd.

Now listen and check your answers.

Asking how to spell words.

Teacher:	Student:	Teacher:
Bangkok	How do you spell that?	"B-A-N-G-K-O-K"

**FOCUS**

Listen to the names and places. Ask how to spell them.
Write them.

1. ....   4. ....

2. ....   5. ....

3. ....   6. ....

Listen.

1. A: It's at 469 Beale Street.
   A: Yes, that's right.

   B: **Did you say** Beale Street?

2. A: It's at 469 Beale Street.
   A: 469 Beale Street.

   B: **Could you repeat that?**
   B: Thank you.

3. A: It's at 469 Beale Street.
   A: B-E-A-L-E.

   B: **How do you spell** Beale?
   B: Thank you.

Practice the conversations.

HINT ☞

Prepositions:
in is used for large areas (countries, states, cities)
I live **in** *Japan. My friend lives* **in** *Rio de Janeiro.*
on is used for streets. *Her apartment is* **on** *Fifth Avenue.*
at is used for street addresses. *He lives* **at** *4915 Barlow Blvd.*

FOCUS

Read the sentences. Write the correct preposition.

1. He lives .... Fourth Street.

2. They are staying .... 458 North Spring Road.

3. He lives .... Pusan, Korea.

4. She has an apartment .... River Street.

5. He used to live .... Vancouver.

Many parts of an address have short forms—abbreviations.
Write the abbreviations.

street	=	....	North	=	....
avenue	=	....	South	=	....
road	=	....	East	=	....
apartment	=	....	West	=	....
building	=	....			

You are A **Your partner is B**

A: Does it have a B? B: No.

A: Does it have an S? B: Yes, it does.

A: Where is it? B: It's the 1st (2nd or 3rd) letter.
(or)
There are two. The 5th and 6th letters are "O".

1. Guess the words. B is thinking of a word. Ask the letters. Write the words.

a. S C _ _ _ _
    1   2   3   4   5   6

b. _ _ _ _ _ _
    1   2   3   4   5   6

c. _ _ _ _ _ _
    1   2   3   4   5   6

d. _ _ _ _ _ _ _
    1   2   3   4   5   6   7

e. _ _ _ _ _ _
    1   2   3   4   5   6

2. B will guess these words:

a. apartment   b. hotel   c. Thailand   d. street   e. Brazil

3. Read these addresses. B will write them.

a. The President of the U.S.
   White House
   1600 Pennsylvania Ave.
   Washington, D.C. 20202
   USA

b. Madonna
   United Fan Mail Service
   9056 Santa Monica Blvd.
   W. Hollywood, California 90046
   USA

4. Write the addresses B says. Check all the information.
For example: How do you spell that? Did you say ....?

a..
....
....
....

b..
....
....
....

5. Fill out this card for B. Ask for the information.

Friends of the
Name_____
Address_____
City_____ Postal code_____
Phone_____
Membership Card

JUST FOR FUN

You and your partner are taking a trip around the world together. You must go to a place that starts with each letter of the alphabet (except X) and you must go in order. Take turns. You can each say "pass" for one letter.

Example:

A: Let's go to **A**laska.   (**A**)
B: OK. Then, let's go to **B**angkok. (**B**)
A: OK. Then, let's go to **C**hina.   (**C**)
B: Next, let's visit **D**enmark.   (**D**)

PAGE B

Pair Practice

Your partner is A

You are B

A: Does it have a B? B: No.

A: Does it have an S? B: Yes, it does.

A: Where is it? B: It's the 1st (2nd, or 3rd) letter. (or) There are two. The 5th and 6th letters are "O".

1. Think of this word: SCHOOL
A will ask about the letters. A will guess these words:
a. school b. Avenue c. Robert d. Chicago e. Quebec

2. Ask A about the letters. Guess these words.

a. A P ___ ___ ___ ___ ___ ___ ___
    1 2 3 4 5 6 7 8 9

b. ___ ___ ___ ___ ___
    1 2 3 4 5

c. ___ ___ ___ ___ ___ ___ ___ ___
    1 2 3 4 5 6 7 8

d. ___ ___ ___ ___ ___ ___
    1 2 3 4 5 6

e. ___ ___ ___ ___ ___ ___
    1 2 3 4 5 6

3. Write the addresses A says. Check all the information.
For example: How do you spell that? Did you say ....?

a... b...

....

....

....

4. Read these addresses. A will write them.

a. Elvis Presley Graceland Mansion
   3734 Elvis Presley Blvd.
   Memphis, Tennessee 38116
   USA

b. Museum of Modern Art
   11 West 53rd. St.
   New York, New York 10019
   USA

5. Fill out this card for A. Ask for the information.

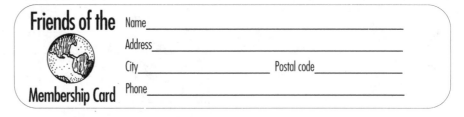

Friends of the Membership Card
Name_____
Address_____
City_____ Postal code_____
Phone_____

You and your partner are taking a trip around the world together. You must go to a place that starts with each letter of the alphabet (except X) and you must go in order. Take turns. You can each say "pass" for one letter.

Example:

A: Let's go to **A**laska. (**A**)
B: OK. Then, let's go to **B**angkok. (**B**)
A: OK. Then, let's go to **C**hina (**C**)
B: Next, let's visit **D**enmark. (**D**)

Social Conversation

Greeting, inviting, suggesting.

CONVERSATION GUIDE

Listen.

- *Greeting*
  1. A: Hi, Emi. **How are you doing?**   B: Pretty good. How about you?
     A: Not bad. **How was your weekend?**   B: It was great. I went to a concert.

  2. A: Hello, Kent. **How are you?**   B: Fine, thanks. And you?

- *Inviting*
  3. A: **Would you like to** go to a movie Saturday? B: That sounds good.

  4. A: **Do you want to** go to a concert Friday? B: Sorry, I have to work. Maybe another time.

     A: OK.

- *Suggesting*
  5. A: **How about** the new Micky Rourke film? B: Great. I love his movies.

  6. A: **Let's go** to the jazz concert. B: Well, I don't really like jazz. How about something else?

     A: OK.

Practice the conversations.

GroupRESPONSE

Listen. Choose an answer. Circle the letter. Say your answer.

1. a. I went to a concert.
   b. I'm reading a book.
   c. Fine, thanks. And you?

2. a. Sorry, I have to work.
   b. Fine, thanks. And you?
   c. Great. I love movies.

3. a. How about you?
   b. Great. I love dancing.
   c. I don't really like steak.

4. a. Sorry, I have to work.
      Maybe another time.
   b. That sounds good.
   c. Great. I went to a baseball game.

5. a. I don't really like heavy metal.
   b. I'm watching TV.
   c. Pretty good. How about you?

6. a. That sounds good.
   b. Fine, thanks. And you?
   c. I went to a concert.

7. a. Pretty good. How about you?
   b. I don't really like Indian food. How
      about Chinese?
   c. How about the Tom Cruise film?

8. a. That sounds good.
   b. I went to a restaurant.
   c. Pretty good. How about you?

Remember!

Close your book. Work with a partner.
How many of the phrases in **bold** can you remember? Write them.

The Small Talk Game

START

HOLIDAYS
Say the names of three holidays.

FAMILY
How many brothers and sisters do you have?

FREE TIME
What free time activity do you like?

MUSIC
What kind of music do you like?

HOLIDAYS
Which holiday do you like the best?

WHAT TIME?
Ask your partners:
What time did you go to bed last night?

ACTIVITIES
What are three activities that you do every day?
When do you do them?

GREETING
Say: *Hi. How are you?*
All partners, please answer.

Hi...

WHAT TIME?
Ask your partners:
What time did you get up today?
Who got up the earliest today?

It's about...

NUMBERS
What's the population of your country?

DATES
What is an important year in the history of your country? Say the year.
Why is it important?

Let's...

SUGGESTING
Say: *Let's...*
Partner, please answer.

SPELLING
Think of a difficult name or word.
Ask your partners:
Who can spell it?

Can you spell...?

SUGGESTING
Say: *How about...?*
Partner, please answer.

DATES
What is an important date in history?

How about...?

This is a Conversation Game.

Work in groups of four.
Use one book for the game board.
Each person needs a small object to mark his or her place.

Close your eyes.
Touch the "How Many Spaces" box with a pencil.
Move that number of spaces.

HOW MANY SPACES?

1 4 2 1 4 5 2 3 2 1
5 3 2 2 1 3 4 2 4 2
2 1 4 3 2 1 5 1 2 3
1 3 4 2 4 2 5 3 2 2
4 1 3 4 2 1 3 4 2 4

Read the information out loud.
If you can answer the question in English, you get 2 points.

Take turns.
Each person answers at least 4 questions.
The first person to get 10 points is the winner.

INVITATION
Invite a partner to go to a movie.
Partner, please answer.

Would you?

NUMBERS
How many students are there in this class?
Say the number.

How are you doing?

Do you want to...?

NAMES
Say the name of everyone in your group.

SPORTS
What sport do you like?
Give one reason.

GREETING
Say:
How are you doing?
Partner, please answer.

INVITATION
Invite a partner to go somewhere.
Partner, please answer.

?

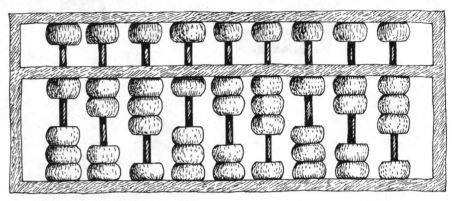

Reading large numbers.

| HINT | Think in 3's! | million ↓ | thousand ↓ |

1 2 3 , 1 2 3 , 1 2 3

"One hundred twenty three million, one hundred twenty three thousand, one hundred twenty three!"

FOCUS

Write the words. Then write the numbers.

a. Two .... , four .... thirty-two .... ,
    nine .... twenty-one.

    In numbers: 2,432,921

b. Thirty-two .... , seventy-four .... , one.

    In numbers: ....

c. Three .... , sixty-seven .... ,
    seven .... twelve.

    In numbers: ....,..................

FOCUS

Write the numbers. Don't write the sentences.

1. ....   6. ....

2. ....   7. ....

3. ....   8. ....

4. ....   9. ....

5. ....   10. ....

CONVERSATION GUIDE

Listen.

1. A: What's the population of
      Australia?
   A: What is the population of
      Australia?

   B: Could you repeat that?

   B: It's 16,500,000.

2. A: What's the population of
      Singapore?
   A: Did you say 2,060,000?

   B: It's 2,600,000.

   B: No. 2,600,000.

Practice the conversations.

GroupRESPONSE

Look at the chart. Listen to the questions. Say the answers.

COUNTRY	POPULATION
Australia	16,500,000
Brazil	119,098,992
Japan	117,057,485
Singapore	2,600,000
United States	226,594,725
United Kingdom	57,100,000

You are A **Your partner is B**

What is the population of Canada?

Twenty six million ...

1. Ask B for the missing information. Write it on the chart.

What is the population of Canada? What is the .... ?

COUNTRY	POPULATION		LARGEST CITY	(POPULATION)
Canada	....		Toronto	(3,500,000)
Mexico	89,500,000		....	
Taiwan	....		Taipei	(2,750,000)
Argentina	32,600,000		....	
Thailand	....		Bangkok	(5,600,000)

2. Answer B's questions.

3. How many?

This is a guessing game. Read your questions (*1, *3, *5). B will guess the answers. Is B right? Listen to B's questions. Guess. Check (✓) the correct answer.

* 1. How many islands are there in Japan?
   Answer: over 3,000

2. ☐ about 1,300   ☐ over 13,000   ☐ almost 17,500

* 3. How many horses are there in the world?
   Answer: about 75,000,000

4. ☐ about 49,800,000   ☐ over 83,000,000   ☐ almost 127,000,000

* 5. How many people are there in New Zealand?
   Answer: over 3,300,000

6. ☐ about 3,300,000   ☐ almost 15,790,000   ☐ over 60,000,000

JUST FOR FUN

Work with your partner. Use hand signals for these numbers. (Don't say anything.) Example: 7,308

a. 1,304   b. 13,468   c. 987,654   d. 7,439,001
B will write and say the numbers.
Write B's numbers. Say them.

| Your partner is A | You are B |

How many people are there in Mexico?

89,500,000.

1. Answer A's questions.

COUNTRY	POPULATION	LARGEST CITY (POPULATION)
Canada	26,100,000	....
Mexico	....	Mexico City (21,000,000)
Taiwan	21,450,000	....
Argentina	....	Buenos Aires (10,500,000)
Thailand	55,790,000	....

2. Ask A for the missing information. Write it on the chart.

What is the population of Mexico? What is the .... ?

3. How many?

This is a guessing game. Listen to A's questions. Guess the answers. Check (✓) the correct answer. Read your questions (*2, *4, *6). A will guess the answers. Is A right?

1. ☐ nearly 30   ☐ about 300   ☐ over 3,000

* 2. How many islands are there in Indonesia?
     Answer: over 13,000

3. ☐ nearly 578,000   ☐ almost 48,000,000   ☐ about 75,000,000

* 4. How many cats are there in the United States?
     Answer: about 49,800,000

5. ☐ over 3,300,000   ☐ about 13,300,000   ☐ almost 33,000,000

* 6. How many sheep are there in New Zealand?
     Answer: over 60,000,000

JUST FOR FUN

Work with your partner. Use hand signals for the numbers. (Don't say anything.) Example: 7,308

7 , 3 0 8

Write and say A's numbers.
Give hand signals for these numbers:
a. 1,802   b .12,864   c. 798,465   d. 4,793,010
A will write and say them.

Look at the groups. Can you find two more examples for each group?

drinks

food

....

Match the words to their groups.

A *sweater* is a type of   animal

A *hammer* is a kind of   furniture

Pizza is a kind of   clothing

A *lion* is a kind of   food

A *chair* is a type of   tool

Listen and check.

What is it made from? Listen. Write the words.

HINT   **If you don't know, ask.** How do you spell ....?
What does .... mean?

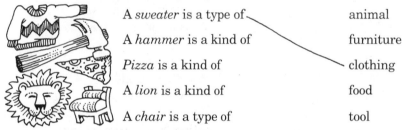

1. 2. 3. 4.

made from   made from   made from   made from

....

....

or ....

....

and ....

CONVERSATION GUIDE

Listen.

1. A: What's lasagne?
   B: It's a food. It's made from pasta, meat, and cheese.

2. A: What's that?
   A: A modem?
   B: It's a modem.
   B: Yes. I use it for sending computer messages.

3. A: What's that?
   A: A llama?
   B: It's a llama.
   B: Yes, they live in South America.

Practice the conversations.

Group RESPONSE

Listen. Which things are they talking about? Say the answers. Number the pictures (1–7).

...... a truck   ...... a watch   ...... a computer   ...... a saw

...... a refrigerator (fridge)   ...... a fax machine   ...... a credit card

Listen. What is being described?

8. ....

9. ....

10. ....

PAGE A

You are A | **Your partner is B**

What does it look like?

It's a kind of animal.

1. What is it? Do not say the names of the objects. Tell B these hints. B will guess.

Hints:

1. It's a kind of animal. It is fairly small. Its fur is usually brown or black.

2. It is made of metal and plastic. It is large. It is used for traveling.

HINT 👉 **If you don't know, ask.** How do you say .... in English?

2. Listen to B's hints. Guess the objects. Write them.

3. .... 4. ....

3. Give hints. B will guess these objects. Listen to B's hints. Guess the other objects. Write them.

5. a jacket 6. ....

7. spaghetti 8. ....

9. a grapefruit 10. ....

11. a magazine 12. ....

13. a dog 14. ....

15. socks 16. ....

4. Find the mistakes. Read this paragraph to B. B will try to find the mistakes.

A camel is a small animal. It has black fur. Camels are used for traveling. They live in the Middle East and North America. Camels can live for a long time without water. What are the mistakes?

Mistakes: Camels are large. They have brown fur. They live in the Middle East and North Africa.

5. Listen to B's paragraph. Find the mistakes. Write them.

....

JUST FOR FUN 👉

Work with B. Play the guessing game at the top of this page. Think of other objects. B will guess. Take turns.

PAGE B

Pair Practice

| Your partner is A | **You are B** |

1. What is it? Listen to A's hints. Guess the objects. Write them.

1. .... 2. ....

What does it look like?

It's a kind of animal.

2. Do not say the names of the objects. Tell A these hints. A will guess.

Hints:

3. It's a type of food.
   It is usually round.
   It is made from flour, eggs, and sugar.

4. It's a kind of clothing.
   It's usually made of cloth or leather.
   It's usually round.

HINT 👉 **If you don't know, ask.** How do you say .... in English?

3. Listen to A's hints. Guess the objects. Write them. Give hints about the other objects. A will guess.

5. .... 6. a banana

7. .... 8. shoes

9. .... 10. a fridge (refrigerator)

11. .... 12. jeans

13. .... 14. a cat

15. .... 16. a boat

4. Listen to A's paragraph. There are some mistakes. Find the mistakes. Write them.

....

5. Read this paragraph to A. A will try to find the mistakes.

Pizza is a type of food. It is usually round. Pizza crust is made from flour, salt, coffee, and water. The crust is covered with sauce, vegetables, meat, metal, and cheese. Sometimes, spices are used to give the pizza flavor. What are the mistakes?

Mistakes: Pizza crust isn't made from coffee. You never make a pizza from metal!

JUST FOR FUN

Work with A. Play the guessing game at the top of this page. Think of other objects. A will guess. Take turns.

Pronunciation

Listen. Repeat the phrases.

Turn right.
Turn left.
Go straight.
It's on the corner.
It's in the middle of the street.
It's across from the house.

It's around the corner from the bank.
It's between two houses.
It's on the left of the house.
It's next to a house.
It's on the right of the house.

FOCUS

Look at the pictures. Can you write the words?

1.

The park is .... the bank.

It's .... the bank and

the supermarket.

2.

The hospital is to ....

.... the bookstore.

It's in .... of the block.

3.

The department store is ....

.... the shoe store.

It's .... of

Second Avenue and Main Street.

4.

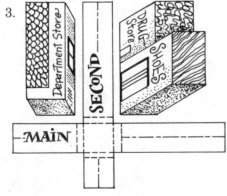

The music store is ....

.... from the library.

Turn .... at the signal.

Now listen to the conversations. Write the words.

40

Listen.

1. A: Where's the bank?

   A: Between the theater and
   the video shop. Thanks.

2. A: Excuse me. How do I get to
   the video shop?

   A: Right at the coffeeshop?

   A: On the right or the left?
   A: Thank you.

B: It's **between** the movie theater
and the video shop.

B: You're welcome.

B: **Go down** this street one block.
Turn right at the coffee shop.

B: Yes. It's **in the middle**
of the block.

B: It's on your left.

Practice the conversations.

GroupRESPONSE

Look at the map. Answer the questions. Use these words:

1. between
2. next to
3. across from
4. on the corner of

5. around the corner
6. in the middle of the block
Start at the drug store:
7. Fifth Street / turn / on your
8. Fifth Street / turn / across from

You are A   **Your partner is B**

Ask B how to get to these places. Write the numbers on the map. Answers B's questions. Take turns.

1. the video shop
3. the supermarket
5. department store

7. the music store
9. the library
11. the park

HINT **When you don't understand, ask.**

Did you say .... ?
Could you repeat that?

How do I get to the video shop?

Start at the bus stop and go north on Broadway Avenue for one block, then ...

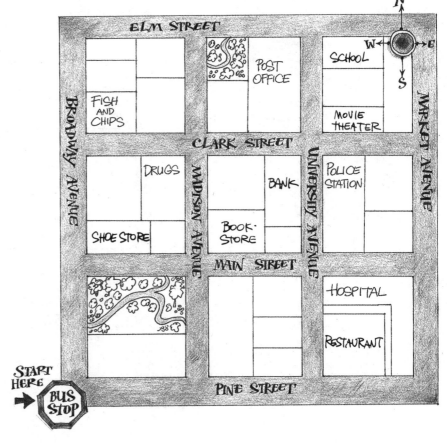

Tell B how to get from your school to:

1. Your favorite restaurant

2. Your favorite store

3. A movie theater

B will draw a map. Then draw a map to the places B tells you about. Think of more places. Continue.

PAGE B

Pair Practice

Your partner is A	You are B

Answers A's questions. Ask A how to get to these places. Write the numbers on the map. Take turns.

2. the bookstore
4. the movie theater
6. the bank

8. the restaurant
10. the school
12. the shoe store

How do I get to the bookstore?

Start at the bus stop and go east on Pine Street for one block then turn left on …

HINT 👉	**When you don't understand, ask.**

Did you say …. ?
Could you repeat that?

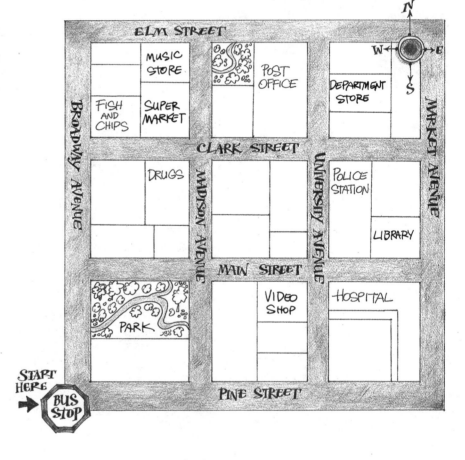

ELM STREET

MUSIC STORE

POST OFFICE

DEPARTMENT STORE

FISH AND CHIPS

SUPER MARKET

BROADWAY AVENUE

CLARK STREET

MARKET AVENUE

DRUGS

MADISON AVENUE

POLICE STATION

UNIVERSITY AVENUE

LIBRARY

MAIN STREET

PARK

VIDEO SHOP

HOSPITAL

START HERE ➡

BUS STOP

PINE STREET

N
W E
S

JUST FOR FUN 👇

Listen to A's directions. Draw a map. Then tell A how to get from your school to these places:

1. Your favorite park
2. Your favorite store
3. A good restaurant

MEGA MANIA

Chez BON

Think of more places. Continue.

Present Actions

CONVERSATION GUIDE

Listen.

1. A: Hello.

   A: Not much. I'm just reading the newspaper and drinking a cup of coffee.
   A: Why?

   A: Thanks for telling me.

   B: Hi, Sara. This is Bob. What are you doing?

   B: Turn on the TV.
   B: There's a rock concert on Channel 8. They're playing some great music.

2. A: Hello.

   A: No, she isn't. She's working right now.
   A: He's at the library. He's studying for a big test.

   B: Hi. This is Kim. Is your sister there?

   B: How about your brother?

   B: Oh, OK. I'll call back later.

Practice the conversations.

GroupRESPONSE

What are these people doing? Say the answers.

1. eat dinner
   drink coffee

2. cook

3. read a book
   listen to music

4. play tennis

5. sing and dance

6. talk on the phone

Listen. Finish the sentences.

1. Peter's drinking .... and reading a ....

2. Where are they .... ?

3. What .... he .... ?

4. She's going ....

5. You're not .... , are you?

Imagine. What are you doing ... ? Answer the questions.

Example: What are you usually doing at 8:00?
You write: watching TV.

6. ....

7. ....

8. ....

Compare answers with your classmates.
Say your answers (6–8).

How many other students gave the same answers?

Write the numbers.   6. .... people

7. .... people

8. .... people

You are A   **Your partner is B**

1. Look at the picture. Who are these people? Ask B.
Answer B's questions.   What's Anne doing?   She's singing.
Who's singing?   Anne.

Write the names on the picture:

Anne   Chris   Dan   Eric   June   Mary   Paul   Steve

Vocabulary check:

cooking

drinking coffee

eating

fighting

laughing

listening to music

playing with a dog

reading a ....

singing

sitting in a chair

sleeping

talking to ....

talking on the phone

throwing a ball

watching TV

2. Do these actions. B will guess what you're doing.

Are you touching your desk? Yes. (That's right.) *or* No.

1. Touch your desk.   2. Look at the teacher.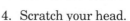

3. Clap your hands.   4. Scratch your head.

5. Whistle.   6. Smile.

3. Guess what B is doing.

HINT ☞   **If you don't know a word, ask B.**
How do you say .... in English?

JUST FOR FUN   Work with B. What are people in your class doing right now? Write the actions.
  • Tomiko is speaking English.
  • Ami is using her dictionary.
  • Mr. Hayes is walking around the room.
How many actions can you and your partner see?

Your partner is A   You are B

1. Look at the picture. Who are these people? Ask A. Answer A's questions.

What's Aaron doing?   He's singing.
Who's the boy who is singing?   That's Aaron.

Write the names on the picture:

Aaron   Debbie   Eli   Jean   Joel   Kay   Mike   Peter

Vocabulary check:

cooking
drinking coffee
eating
fighting
laughing
listening to music
playing with a dog
reading a ....
singing
sitting in a chair
sleeping
talking to ....
talking on the phone
throwing a ball
watching TV

2. Guess what A is doing.

Are you writing your name? That's right. (or) No, I'm doing something else.

HINT 👉   **If you dont know a word, ask A.**
                          How do you say .... in English?

3. Do these actions. A will guess what you're doing.

1. Write your name.
2. Open and close your eyes.
3. Wave at A.
4. Raise your hand.
5. Touch your book.
6. Hold your pen in your left hand.

 JUST FOR FUN

Work with A. What are people in your class doing right now? Write the actions.
   • Tomiko is speaking English.
   • Ami is using her dictionary.
   • Mr. Hayes is walking around the room.
How many actions can you and your partner see?

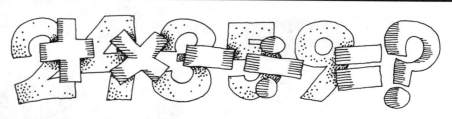

GroupRESPONSE

Math Functions. Say these words:

+   plus   x   times
−   minus   ÷   divided by   =   equals (or) is

Say these problems. Write the verbs.

4 + 5 = 9   Four .... five equals nine.

15 ÷ 10 = 1.5   Fifteen .... by ten is one point five.

69 − 68 = 1   Sixty-nine .... sixty-eight .... one.

9 x 8 = 72   Nine .... eight is seventy-two.

Math Verbs. Say these words:

+   add   −   subtract   x   multiply   ÷   divide

Say these directions. Write the verbs.

4 + 5   .... 4 and 5.

25 − 5   .... 5 from 25.

8 x 11   .... 8 by 11.

5 ÷ 10   .... 5 by 10.

FOCUS

Listen. Write the problems. Find the answers. Say them.

HINT **When you don't understand, ask.**
Did you say **13** or **30**? Could you repeat that?

1. ....   6. ....

2. ....   7. ....

3. ....   8. ....

4. ....   9. ....

5. ....   10. ....

48

CONVERSATION GUIDE

Listen.

1. A: The bill is $27.
   A: That's $6.75 each?

   B: There are four of us, so...
   B: Right.

2. A: How much are these socks?
   A: I'll take 3 pairs.

   B: They're $4.50 a pair.
   B: OK, that's $13.50.

Practice the conversations.

FOCUS

Listen. Follow the instructions.
You'll hear each step two times.

Think of a number between 10 and 1,000.

Your answer should be ....

You are A   **Your partner is B**

What's four
plus fifteen?

Nineteen.

1. Read these problems to B. B will find the answers as fast as possible. Are the answers correct?

1. What's 4 + 15 ?   2. What's 80 – 14 ?   3. What's 18 x 2 ?

2. B will read three problems. Write the problems. Find the answers quickly. Say the answers.

1. ....   2. ....   3. ....

3. Read this problem. Listen to the answer. Is it correct?

Write 145.   Multiply it by 6.   Divide it by 3.   Add 14.

What's the answer?   *(Answer: 304)*

4. Listen to the problem. Write the answer: ....

Magic!

5. Math Magic, part 1. Read this problem.

Write your age.   ....

Multiply by 12.   ....

Subtract 8.   ....

Divide by 4.   ....

Add 2.   ....

Divide by 3.   ....

The answer should be your age.

Magic!

6. Math Magic, part 2. Listen to B. Do the problem.

Write the answer. ....

JUST
FOR
FUN

Work with your partner. One person says a math
problem. The other tries to answer it quickly. Continue.
Take turns.

Pair Practice

| Your partner is A | You are B |

What's ninety divided by thirty?

Three.

1. Write the problems. Find the answers quickly. Say the answers.

1. .... 2. .... 3. ....

2. Read these problems to A. A will find the answers as fast as possible. Are the answers correct?

1. What's 90 ÷ 30 ?   2. What's 12 x 7 ?   3. What's 9 + 8 ?

3. Listen to the problem. Write the answer: ....

4. Read this problem. Listen to the answer. Is it correct?

Start with 400.   Multiply it by 32.   Subtract 68.   Divide it by 3.

What's the answer?   *(Answer: 4,244)*

Magic!

5. Math Magic, part 1. Listen to A. Do the problem.

Write the answer: ....

Magic!

6. Math Magic, part 2. Read this problem.

Write the first three numbers of your phone number.	....
Multiply the number by 2.	....
Add 5.	....
Multiply by 50.	....
Add your age.	....
Add 365.	....
Subtract 615.	....

The answer should be the first three numbers of your phone number and your age.

JUST FOR FUN

Work with your partner. One person says a math problem. The other tries to answer it quickly. Continue. Take turns.

CONVERSATION GUIDE

Responding, giving advice, requesting.

Listen.

- *Responding*

  Good news:
  1. A: I got an A on the test.   B: **That's wonderful.**
  2. A: I got a new job.   B: **Great!**
  3. A: I won the contest.   B: **I'm glad to hear that.**

  Bad news:
  4. A: My brother is really sick.   B: **I'm sorry to hear that.**
  5. A: I failed my math test.   B: **That's too bad.**
  6. A: I lost my wallet.   B: **That's terrible!**

  Neutral:
  (not good or bad)
  7. A: I went to the movies last night.   B: **Really?**
  8. A: I called Lee last night.   B: **Uh-huh.**

- *Giving Advice*
  9. A: I have a headache.   B: **Why don't you** take some aspirin?
  10. A: I'm really tired today.   B: **You should** go to bed earlier.

- *Requesting*
  11. A: **Could you** help me?   B: **Sure.**
  12. A: **Can I borrow** your pen?   B: **Sorry.** I'm using it.

Practice the conversations.

GroupRESPONSE

 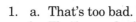

Listen. Choose an answer. Say it and circle the letter.

1. a. That's too bad.
   b. That's wonderful.
   c. Sorry, I'm busy now.

2. a. You should take some aspirin.
   b. That's great.
   c. That's terrible.

3. a. Uh-huh.
   b. That's too bad.
   c. Why don't you call her?

4. a. Really?
   b. Great!
   c. Sure. Here's five dollars.

5. a. I'm sorry to hear that.
   b. That's wonderful.
   c. Sure. Here it is.

6. a. I'm glad to hear that.
   b. I'm sorry to hear that.
   c. Sorry, I'm busy now.

7. a. That's terrible.
   b. Great!
   c. Sorry, I'm using it.

8. a. That's wonderful.
   b. You should study more.
   c. Why don't you go to the doctor?

9. a. Why don't you ask him?
   b. Really?
   c. Sure. Here you are.

10. a. That's great.
    b. You should take some aspirin.
    c. Sorry, I'm using it.

Remember!

Close your book. Work with a partner.

How many of the sentences and phrases in **bold** can you remember? Write them.

The Small Talk Game

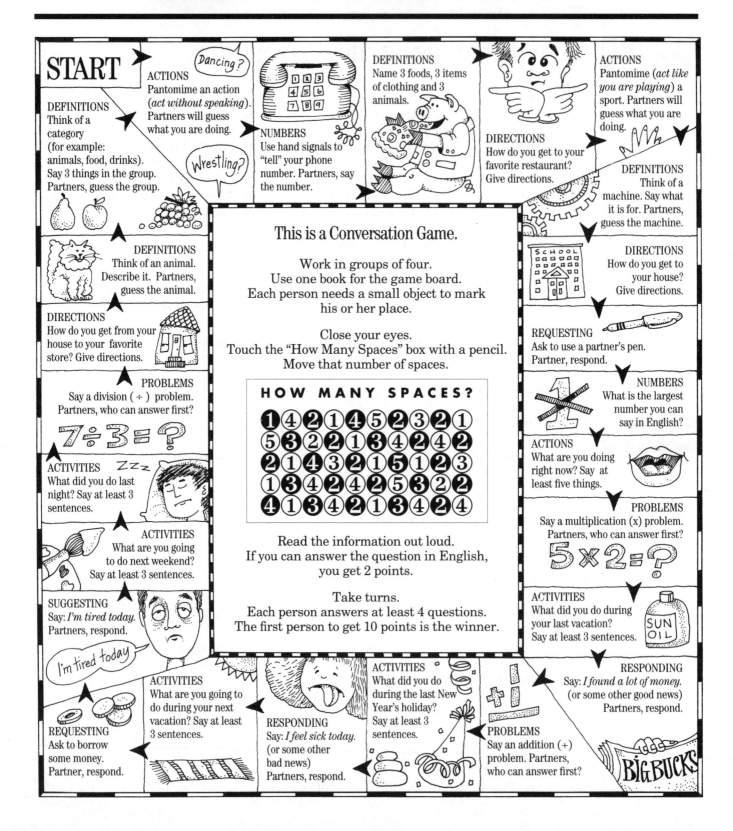

START

ACTIONS
Pantomime an action (*act without speaking*). Partners will guess what you are doing.

Dancing?

Wrestling?

DEFINITIONS
Think of a category (for example: animals, food, drinks). Say 3 things in the group. Partners, guess the group.

NUMBERS
Use hand signals to "tell" your phone number. Partners, say the number.

DEFINITIONS
Name 3 foods, 3 items of clothing and 3 animals.

DIRECTIONS
How do you get to your favorite restaurant? Give directions.

ACTIONS
Pantomime (*act like you are playing*) a sport. Partners will guess what you are doing.

DEFINITIONS
Think of a machine. Say what it is for. Partners, guess the machine.

DEFINITIONS
Think of an animal. Describe it. Partners, guess the animal.

DIRECTIONS
How do you get to your house? Give directions.

DIRECTIONS
How do you get from your house to your favorite store? Give directions.

REQUESTING
Ask to use a partner's pen. Partner, respond.

PROBLEMS
Say a division (÷) problem. Partners, who can answer first?

$7 ÷ 3 = ?$

NUMBERS
What is the largest number you can say in English?

ACTIVITIES
What did you do last night? Say at least 3 sentences.

ACTIONS
What are you doing right now? Say at least five things.

ACTIVITIES
What are you going to do next weekend? Say at least 3 sentences.

PROBLEMS
Say a multiplication (x) problem. Partners, who can answer first?

$5 × 2 = ?$

SUGGESTING
Say: *I'm tired today.* Partners, respond.

I'm tired today

ACTIVITIES
What did you do during your last vacation? Say at least 3 sentences.

SUN OIL

ACTIVITIES
What are you going to do during your next vacation? Say at least 3 sentences.

RESPONDING
Say: *I feel sick today.* (or some other bad news) Partners, respond.

ACTIVITIES
What did you do during the last New Year's holiday? Say at least 3 sentences.

RESPONDING
Say: *I found a lot of money.* (or some other good news) Partners, respond.

REQUESTING
Ask to borrow some money. Partner, respond.

PROBLEMS
Say an addition (+) problem. Partners, who can answer first?

BIG BUCKS

This is a Conversation Game.

Work in groups of four.
Use one book for the game board.
Each person needs a small object to mark his or her place.

Close your eyes.
Touch the "How Many Spaces" box with a pencil.
Move that number of spaces.

HOW MANY SPACES?

1	4	2	1	4	5	2	3	2	1
5	3	2	2	1	3	4	2	4	2
2	1	4	3	2	1	5	1	2	3
1	3	4	2	4	2	5	3	2	2
4	1	3	4	2	1	3	4	2	4

Read the information out loud.
If you can answer the question in English, you get 2 points.

Take turns.
Each person answers at least 4 questions.
The first person to get 10 points is the winner.

CONVERSATION GUIDE

Listen.

1. A: What did you do last weekend?
   A: I went shopping. I bought some skis.
   A: Next weekend.

   B: I visited my parents. How about you?
   B: When are you going skiing?

> **HINT** **Most verbs use "ed" in the past. Some have new forms:** buy - bought
> go - went, eat - ate, see - saw, do - did, ride - rode, write - wrote

2. A: Were you in class today?
   A: Are you going to be there tomorrow?

   B: No, I was sick.
   B: No, I'm going to go to the doctor.

> **HINT** **"Going to" + verb** (I'm going to play tennis on Saturday)
> is the most common way to show a future action.

Practice the conversations.

GroupRESPONSE

Listen. Check (✓) the times. Say the sentences:

1. watch TV
   ☐ LAST NIGHT
   ☐ TONIGHT

2. swim
   ☐ LAST SUNDAY
   ☐ NEXT SUNDAY

3. dance
   ☐ LAST WEEKEND
   ☐ NEXT WEEKEND

4. visit friends
   ☐ YESTERDAY
   ☐ TOMORROW

5. go to Hawaii
   ☐ LAST SUMMER
   ☐ THIS SUMMER

6. eat dinner
   ☐ AT 6 LAST NIGHT
   ☐ AT 6 TONIGHT

7. study
   ☐ LAST NIGHT
   ☐ TONIGHT

8. ski
   ☐ LAST MONTH
   ☐ NEXT MONTH

9. write some letters
   ☐ YESTERDAY AFTERNOON
   ☐ THIS AFTERNOON

10. shop
   ☐ YESTERDAY MORNING
   ☐ TOMORROW MORNING

Pronunciation

The "ed" on a past tense verb makes different sounds. Listen. Check (✓) the sound. Say the words.

1. called   ☐ / d /   ☐ / t /   ☐ / ɪd /
2. danced   ☐ / d /   ☐ / t /   ☐ / ɪd /
3. played   ☐ / d /   ☐ / t /   ☐ / ɪd /
4. shopped   ☐ / d /   ☐ / t /   ☐ / ɪd /
5. studied   ☐ / d /   ☐ / t /   ☐ / ɪd /
6. visited   ☐ / d /   ☐ / t /   ☐ / ɪd /
7. watched   ☐ / d /   ☐ / t /   ☐ / ɪd /

FOCUS

Listen to the questions. Give answers about yourself.

1. ....

2. ....

3. ....

4. ....

5. ....

Compare answers with your classmates. Say your answers.
How many other students gave the same answers?
Write the numbers.

1. .... people
2. .... people
3. .... people
4. .... people
5. .... people

You are A **Your partner is B**

Where did she go?   She went to …

1. Jan took a vacation. Find out what she did. Ask B. Write the information on the chart.

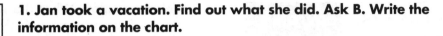

HINT 👉 **Most verbs use "ed" in the past. Some have new forms:** buy - bought go - went, eat - ate, see - saw, do - did, ride - rode, write - wrote

Jan

Place ....
Where did she go?

With ....
Who did she go with?

Activity ....
What else did she do?

Eat ....
What did she eat?

2. Kent is planning his weekend. What is he going to do? Answer B's questions.

Kent

Saturday night
go to a restaurant
and then see a movie

Sunday afternoon
play tennis with
his brother

Sunday night
do his homework

3. Ask B these questions. Write the answers.

1. What did you do last weekend? ....

2. Who were you with? ....

3. Where did you go on your most interesting vacation? ....

4. Who were you with? ....

5. What did you see? ....

6. What are you going to do next weekend? ....

7. Will you go anywhere special? ....

8. What are you going to do after class today? ....

JUST
FOR
FUN

Find at least three things you and B both did last weekend.
Find at least three things you're both going to do this weekend.

Your partner is A	You are B

What is he going to do?

He's going to ...

1. Jan took a vacation. What did she do? Answer A's questions.

Jan

went to San Francisco with a friend

visited Chinatown and then rode the cable cars

ate a lot of seafood

2. Kent is planning his weekend. Find out what he is going to do. Ask A. Write the information on the chart.

HINT 👉	Most verbs use "ed" in the past. Some have new forms: buy - bought go - went, eat - ate, see - saw, do - did, ride - rode, write - **wrote**

Kent

Activity ....
What is he going to do Saturday night?

Then ....
What is he going to do after that?

Sport ....
What is he going to do Sunday afternoon?

With ....
Who will he play with?

Sunday night ....
What is he going to do Sunday night?

3. Ask A these questions. Write the answers.

1. What did you do last weekend? ....

2. Who were you with? ....

3. Where did you go on your most interesting vacation? ....

4. Who were you with? ....

5. What did you see? ....

6. What are you going to do next weekend? ....

7. Will you go anywhere special? ....

8. What are you going to do after class today? ....

JUST
FOR
FUN
👉

Find at least three things you and A both did last weekend.
Find at least three things you're both going to do this weekend.

Pronunciation

Listen. Say the words.

Hair color
- brown
- black
- blond
- gray

Eye color
- brown
- blue
- green

She's tall.
She's thin.

He's short.
He's heavy.

She has long
hair. Her hair
is wavy.

His hair is
short. He has
curly hair.

She has straight,
shoulder-
length hair.

He's bald.

She's got a
ponytail.

He has a
moustache.

He has a beard.

She's wearing
glasses.

Group RESPONSE

Which picture? Listen. Number the pictures (1–9).

A.

D.

G.

B.

E.

H.

C.

F.

I.

Listen.

1. A: Do you know Naomi Kato?

   B: I'm not sure. What does she look like?

   A: She's got wavy, shoulder-length hair. She has glasses, too.

   B: Is she tall?

   A: Yes. Tall and thin.

   B: I think I know her.

2. A: Do you know Jim Wood?

   B: I'm not sure. What does he look like?

   A: Well, he has curly blond hair and a moustache.

   B: Is he tall?

   A: No. He's short and a little heavy.

   B: Um, I don't think I know him.

Practice the conversations.

FOCUS

Listen to the questions. Write answers about yourself.

Example: Question 1.   Is your hair brown?

           You write: Yes, it is. (or)

                         No, my hair is black.

1. ....

2. ....

3. ....

4. ....

5. ....

6. ....

Compare answers with your classmates. Say your answers.

How many other students gave the same answers? Write the numbers.

1. .... people   4. .... people

2. .... people   5. .... people

3. .... people   6. .... people

PAGE A

| You are A | Your partner is B |

Is his hair long or short?

It's short.

1. Tell B what these people look like. Answer B's questions.

Ms. Roberts   Sue   Kevin   Dr. Chung   Matt   Mr. Wells

2. Ask about these people. Write their names on their pictures.
The people: Jill, Mr. Lima, Amy, Mr. Porter, Hiro, Ms. Farmer.

| HINT ☞ | **Ask more than one question about each person:**
What does Jill look like? Is her hair long or short?
Is it straight? Does she have glasses? |

3. Look at B's page. Check B's answers.

JUST FOR FUN

Describe people in your class. Don't say their names.
B will guess. Take turns. Guess the people B describes.

Your partner is A

You are B

1. Ask about the people. Write their names on their pictures.
The people: Ms. Roberts, Sue, Kevin, Dr. Chung, Matt, Mr. Wells.

HINT 👉 **Ask more than one question about each person:**
What does Ms. Roberts look like? Is her hair long or short?
Is it straight? Does she have glasses?

Is his hair long or short?   It's short.

2. Tell A what these people look like. Answer A's questions.

Jill   Mr. Lima   Amy   Mr. Porter   Hiro   Ms. Farmer

3. Look at A's page. Check A's answers.

JUST FOR FUN

Describe people in your class. Don't say their names.
A will guess. Take turns. Guess the people A describes.

CHOICE

Do you like to do these things? Circle the ones you like. Cross out (X) the ones you don't like. Say the words.

camping   cleaning   cooking   doing homework   hiking

listening to music   playing a musical instrument   reading   riding a bicycle   skiing

studying   swimming   taking tests   using a computer

FOCUS

HINT ☞	Some verbs go with another *verb* + ING.	I *enjoy* swimming.
	Other verbs take *to* + *verb*.	I *want to* ski this winter
	Some verbs use either *verb*+ ING or	I *love* watch*ing* movies.
	to + *verb*.	I *love to* watch movies.

Listen. Which do these verbs take? Check (✓) the forms you hear.

Example: A: like
            B: I like skiing.
                I like to ski.

1. like   ☐ ☐ verb+ING   ☐ ☐ to + verb
2. enjoy   ☐ ☐ verb+ING   ☐ ☐ to + verb
3. dislike   ☐ ☐ verb+ING   ☐ ☐ to + verb
4. want   ☐ ☐ verb+ING   ☐ ☐ to + verb
5. learned   ☐ ☐ verb+ING   ☐ ☐ to + verb
6. hope   ☐ ☐ verb+ING   ☐ ☐ to + verb
7. feel like   ☐ ☐ verb+ING   ☐ ☐ to + verb
8. hate   ☐ ☐ verb+ING   ☐ ☐ to + verb

Check your answers.

62

CONVERSATION GUIDE

Listen.

1. A: What are you going to do this weekend?

   B: I want to go camping. I really love hiking in the woods.

   A: Yeah, I like to hike, too.

   B: What are you going to do?

   A: Nothing special. I hope to see a movie.

   B: That sounds like fun.

2. A: Are you doing anything special this weekend?

   B: Yeah. I'm taking a cooking class. I'm learning to make Indian food.

   A: That sounds interesting.

   B: It is. I really enjoy cooking.

   A: Not me. I hate cooking. But I like eating.

Practice the conversations.

FOCUS

Listen. Write the answers about yourself. Don't write the questions.

Example: Question 1. Do you like to ski?
You write: Yes, I like to ski. (or)
No, I don't like to ski.

1. ......*like*... .
2. ......*love*... .
3. ......*hope*... .
4. ......*enjoy*... .
5. ......*feel*... .
6. ......*hate*... .
7. ......*want*... .

PAGE A

You are A	Your partner is B

Do you like listening to classical music?

Yes, I do.

1. Do these people like doing these things? Ask B. Fill in the chart. Answer B's questions.

Does Brian like *to* swim? Yes, he does.
Does Brian like *swimming*? No, he doesn't.

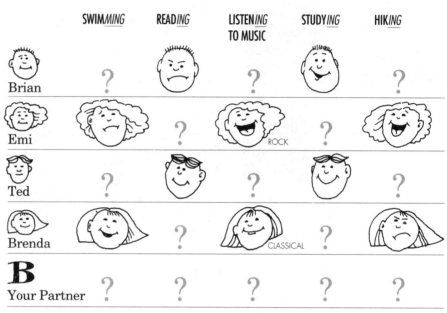

	SWIM*MING*	READ*ING*	LISTEN*ING* TO MUSIC	STUDY*ING*	HIK*ING*
Brian	?		?		?
Emi		?	ROCK	?	
Ted	?		?		?
Brenda		?	CLASSICAL	?	
B Your Partner	?	?	?	?	?

2. Ask B these questions. Answer for yourself: I do, too. (or) I don't. (or) I don't, either. **Circle 'same' or 'different.'**

1. Do you enjoy shopping for clothes? .... same different
2. Do you like listening to classical music? .... same different
3. Do you dislike doing homework? .... same different
4. Do you like watching professional wrestling? .... same different
5. Do you want to get a pet? What kind? .... same different
6. Do you like going to movies? .... same different

Write two more. Ask B.

7. Do you ....? same different
8. Do you ....? same different

JUST FOR FUN

Find at least three more ways you and B are the same.
Find three ways you are different.

| Your partner is A | You are B |

Do you like listening to classical music?

Yes, I do. (or) No, I don't.

1. Do these people like doing these things? Ask A. Fill in the chart. Answer A's questions.

Does Brian like *to* swim?   Yes, he does.
Does Brian like *swimming*?   No, he doesn't.

	SWIM*MING*	READ*ING*	LISTEN*ING* TO MUSIC	STUDY*ING*	HIK*ING*
Brian		?	JAZZ	?	
Emi	?		?		?
Ted		?		?	
Brenda	?		?		?
A Your Partner	?	?	?	?	?

2. Ask A these questions. Answer for yourself: I do, too. (or) I don't. (or) I don't, either. **Circle 'same' or 'different.'**

1. Do you enjoy eating spicy food?   same   different

2. Do you like listening to rock music?   same   different

3. Do you dislike cleaning your room or apartment?   same   different

4. Do you like writing poetry?   same   different

5. Do you want to learn to play a musical instrument? Which one?   same   different

6. Do you like speaking English?   same   different

Write two more. Ask A.

7. Do you .... ?   same   different

8. Do you .... ?   same   different

JUST FOR FUN

Find at least three more ways you and A are the same.
Find three ways you are different.

FOCUS

**Listen to the sentences. Ask how to spell the words.
Say the sentences.**

HINT ☞   **If you don't know, ask:** How do you spell that?
Did you say **b** or **v** ?

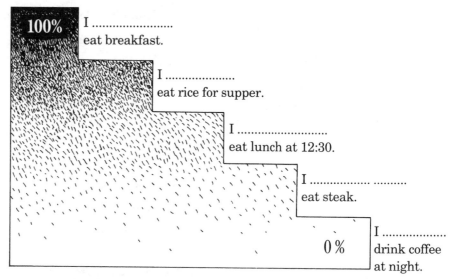

100% I .... eat breakfast.

I .... eat rice for supper.

I .... eat lunch at 12:30.

I .... eat steak.

0 % I .... drink coffee at night.

CONVERSATION GUIDE

Listen.

Do you like reading?

1. A. Do you like reading?

    A: Not me. I usually watch TV.
    A: Sometimes movies.
       Sometimes the news.

    B. Yes. I always read before I go to bed.
    B: What do you watch?

2. A: How often do you listen
       to music?
    A: I hardly ever do. I listen to rock.

    B: Every day. I usually listen to jazz.

Practice the conversations.

GroupRESPONSE

Ask the questions. Listen for the answers. Say the sentences.
Use: *always, usually, sometimes, hardly ever, never.*
Example: ASK: How often does David wake up before 6:30?
LISTEN to the answer: Every day.
SAY: He *always* wakes up before 6:30.

David

1. ASK: How often does he eat breakfast before eight o'clock?
   LISTEN to the answer.
   • SAY: He .... eats breakfast before 8:00.

2. ASK: How often does he listen to music at night?
   LISTEN to the answer.
   • SAY: He .... listens to music at night.

3. ASK: How often does he watch professional wrestling?
   LISTEN to the answer.
   • SAY: He .... watches professional wrestling.

4. ASK: How often does he work more than 10 hours a day?
   LISTEN to the answer.
   • SAY: He .... works more than 10 hours a day.

5. ASK: How often does he read at night?
   LISTEN to the answer.
   • SAY: He .... reads at night.

FOCUS

Listen to the questions. Answer about yourself.

1. I .... *do.* ....

2. ....

3. ....

4. ....

5. ....

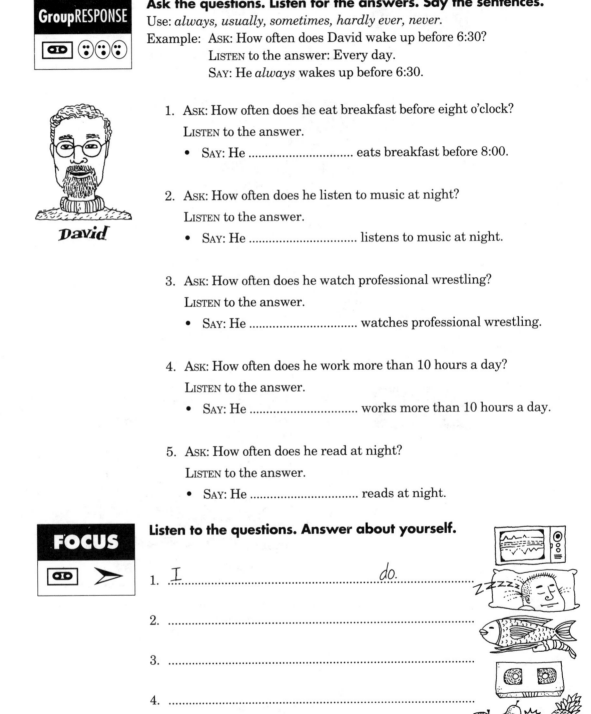

You are A   **Your partner is B**

1. Look at the chart. Ask B. Write the missing information. Answer B's questions.

You: How often does Kim go to the movies on weekends?
B: She usually does. Two or three times a month. How often do you ...

How often do you go to the movies on weekends?

Two or three times a month.

	KIM	LEE	YOUR PARTNER
1. ...go to movies on weekends?	?	Hardly ever (ABOUT TWO TIMES A YEAR)	?
2. ...study after dinner?	Never (SHE STUDIES BEFORE SHE EATS)	?	?
3. ...eat fish for dinner?	?	Usually (ALMOST EVERY DAY)	?
4. ...watch baseball on TV?	Sometimes (SHE WATCHES HER FAVORITE TEAM)	?	?
5. ...listen to music in the evening?	?	Always (TWO OR THREE HOURS EVERY NIGHT)	?

2. Ask B these questions. Write the answers. Who does these things more often? Circle Me, Partner or Same.

How often do you ...	YOUR ANSWER	YOUR PARTNER'S ANSWER	WHO DOES IT MORE?
...eat breakfast before 7:30?	....	....	Me Partner Same
...wake up early on Sunday?	....	....	Me Partner Same
...sleep less than 6 hours?	....	....	Me Partner Same
...read books at night?	....	....	Me Partner Same
...do homework for this class?	....	....	Me Partner Same
...watch TV at night?	....	....	Me Partner Same

HINT   Every day – I **always** do.   Most days – I **usually** do.
A few times – I **sometimes** do. Almost never – I **hardly ever** do.
You don't do it – I **never** do.

JUST FOR FUN

Think of at least five more questions. Ask B.
How many times were your answers the same?

PAGE B

Pair Practice

| Your partner is A | You are B |

**1. Look at the chart. Answer A's questions. Ask A.
Write the missing information.**

A: How often does Kim go to the movies on weekends?
You: She usually does. Two or three times a month. How often do you ...

How often do you go to the movies on weekends?

Two or three times a month.

	KIM	LEE	YOUR PARTNER
1. ...go to movies on weekends?	Usually (TWO OR THREE TIMES A MONTH)	?	?
2. ...study after dinner?	?	Always (ONE OR TWO HOURS EACH NIGHT)	?
3. ...eat fish for dinner?	Hardly ever (SHE DOESN'T LIKE FISH)	?	?
4. ...watch baseball on TV?	?	Never (HIS TV IS BROKEN)	?
5. ...listen to music in the evening?	Sometimes (BUT USUALLY SHE READS)	?	?

**2. Ask A these questions. Write the answers. Who does these
things more often? Circle Me, Partner, or Same.**

How often do you ...	YOUR ANSWER	YOUR PARTNER'S ANSWER	WHO DOES IT MORE?
...eat breakfast before 7:30?	....	....	Me Partner Same
...wake up early on Sunday?	....	....	Me Partner Same
...sleep less than 6 hours?	....	....	Me Partner Same
...read books at night?	....	....	Me Partner Same
...do homework for this class?	....	....	Me Partner Same
...watch TV at night?	....	....	Me Partner Same

| HINT ☞ | Every day – I **always** do.   Most days – I **usually** do.
A few times – I **sometimes** do.   Almost never – I **hardly ever** do.
You don't do it – I **never** do. |

JUST FOR FUN

Think of at least five more questions. Ask A.
How many times were your answers the same?

GroupRESPONSE

Do the actions. Say the words.

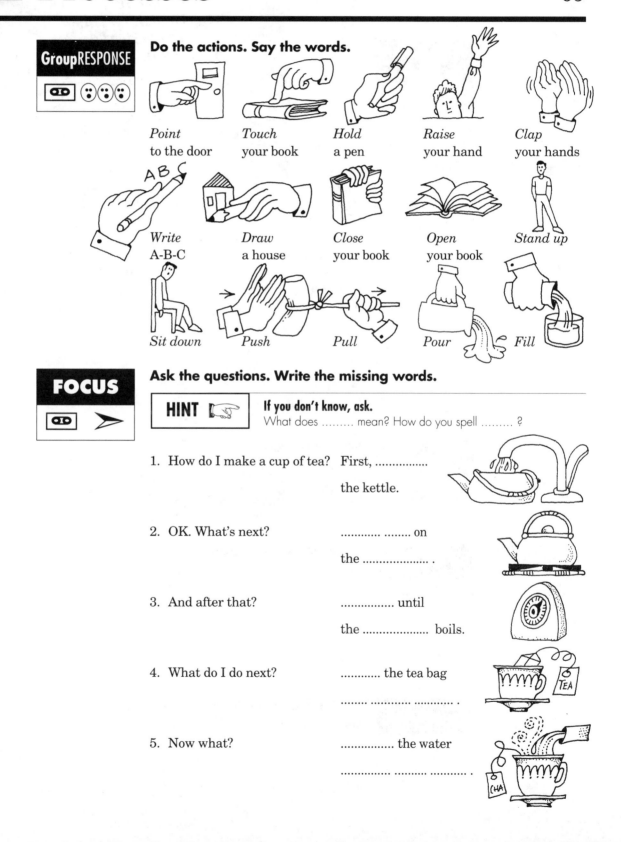

Point
to the door

Touch
your book

Hold
a pen

Raise
your hand

Clap
your hands

Write
A-B-C

Draw
a house

Close
your book

Open
your book

Stand up

Sit down

Push

Pull

Pour

Fill

FOCUS

Ask the questions. Write the missing words.

HINT ☞ **If you don't know, ask.**
What does .... mean? How do you spell .... ?

1. How do I make a cup of tea?   First, ...
   the kettle.

2. OK. What's next?   .... on
   the ....

3. And after that?   .... until
   the .... boils.

4. What do I do next?   .... the tea bag
   ....

5. Now what?   .... the water
   ....

70

CONVERSATION GUIDE

Listen.

A: Excuse me. How does this microwave oven work?
A: OK.
A: How do I do that?
A: I see. What's next?
A: OK.
A: That's all?

A: Thanks.

B: It's easy. First, put the food in.
B: Now, set the temperature control.
B: Just push this button.
B: Set the timer.
B: Last, press the start button.
B: Right. When the bell rings, your food is ready.

Practice the conversation.

Pronunciation

Say these words.

square   rectangle   triangle   circle   line

FOCUS

Listen. Draw the picture.

GroupRESPONSE

Tell how to draw the picture above.
Use this order: *"Draw a large square..."*

1.   2.   3.   4.   5. _____ 6. your name

You are A **Your partner is B**

First, draw a rectangle.

OK. What's next?

1. Tell B how to draw this picture.

1. First, draw a ⬚ .
2. Then, put a ○ on the ⬚ , on the left.
3. After that, put a △ in the ○.
4. Now, put a □ on the ⬚ , next to the ○.
5. Draw a _____ under the ⬚ .
6. Finally, write your name in the □ .

2. Listen to B. Draw the picture.

HINT ☞

Show B you understand: OK. Uh-huh. What's next?
If you don't understand, ask. Could you repeat that?
Did you say right or left?

3. Read the instructions. B will follow them.

1. Close your eyes.
2. Touch your head.
3. Open your eyes.
4. Point to the teacher.

5. Hold your book in your left hand.
6. Raise your hand.
7. Put your hand down.
8. Smile.

Now, B will try to remember these instructions. Say: That's right. (or) No, that isn't next.

4. Follow B's instructions. Then, try to remember the instructions. Say them in order:

1. First, I touched my book.
2. Then I ....
3. After that, I ....
4. Next I ....

5. Then I ....
6. After that, I ....
7. Next I ....
8. Finally, I ....

JUST FOR FUN

Think of a machine you can use or a food you can make.
Examples of machines:
washing machine (for clothes), microwave oven, CD player.
Examples of foods:
curry, "Cup of Noodles" (instant noodles), cheese toast.
Give instructions. B will pantomime the actions (act without speaking).

Pair Practice

First, draw a rectangle.

OK. What's next?

1. Listen to A. Draw the picture.

HINT ☞

Show A you understand: OK. Uh-huh. What's next?
If you don't understand, ask. Could you repeat that?
Did you say right or left?

2. Tell A how to draw this picture.

1. First, draw a □ .
2. Then, put a ○ in the □ .
3. After that, put a △ on the □ .
4. Now, draw a ▭ on the △ .
5. Draw a ── over the ▭ .
6. Finally, write your name to the right of the △ .

3. Follow A's instructions. Then, try to remember the instructions. Say them in order:

1. First, I closed my eyes.
2. Then I ....
3. After that, I ....
4. Next I ....

5. Then I ....
6. After that, I ....
7. Next I ....
8. Finally, I ....

4. Read the instructions. A will follow them.

1. Touch your book.
2. Clap your hands.
3. Close your book.
4. Stand up.

5. Sit down.
6. Hold your pen in your right hand.
7. Point to the door.
8. Put your pen in your pocket.

Now, A will try to remember these instructions. Say: That's right. (or) No, that isn't next.

JUST FOR FUN

Think of a machine you can use or a food you can make.
Examples of machines:
washing machine (for clothes), microwave oven, CD player.
Examples of foods:
curry, "Cup of Noodles" (instant noodles), cheese toast.
Give instructions. A will pantomime the actions
(act without speaking).

CONVERSATION GUIDE

Offering, apologizing, ending a conversation.

Listen.

• *Offering*

1. A: **Would you like** a cup of coffee?   B: Yes, please.
   A: **Do you want** cream and sugar?   B: No, thanks. Just black.

2. A: **How about** something to eat?   B: No, thanks. I'm not hungry.

• *Apologizing*

3. A: What happened?   B: **I'm sorry** I'm late. I missed the bus.

4. A: **Oh, no! I'm really sorry.**   B: That's OK. Don't worry.
   A: Let me clean it up.

• *Ending a Conversation*

5. A: Well, **I need to** get to class.   B: Yeah. **See you** tomorrow.

6. A: It's getting late. **I'd better be going.**   B: Me, too. **Goodbye.**

Practice the conversations.

GroupRESPONSE

Listen. Choose an answer. Say it and circle the letter.

1. a. Cream and sugar, please.
   b. Yes. Cola, please.
   c. I'm really sorry.

2. a. I'll have coffee.
   b. See you tomorrow.
   c. That's OK. Don't worry about it.

3. a. Yes, with sugar, please.
   b. No, thanks.
   c. I missed the bus.

4. a. Yeah. See you tomorrow.
   b. How about coffee?
   c. No, thanks. Just black.

5. a. Don't worry about it.
   b. Ice cream, please.
   c. Vanilla, please.

6. a. No, thanks. I'm not hungry.
   b. Goodbye.
   c. I'm sorry. I missed the train.

7. a. See you next week.
   b. I'm really sorry.
   c. No, thanks. I'm not hungry.

8. a. That's OK.
   b. Yes, please.
   c. Let me clean it up.

Remember!

Close your book. Work with a partner.
How many of the sentences and phrases in **bold** can you remember? Write them.

The Small Talk Game

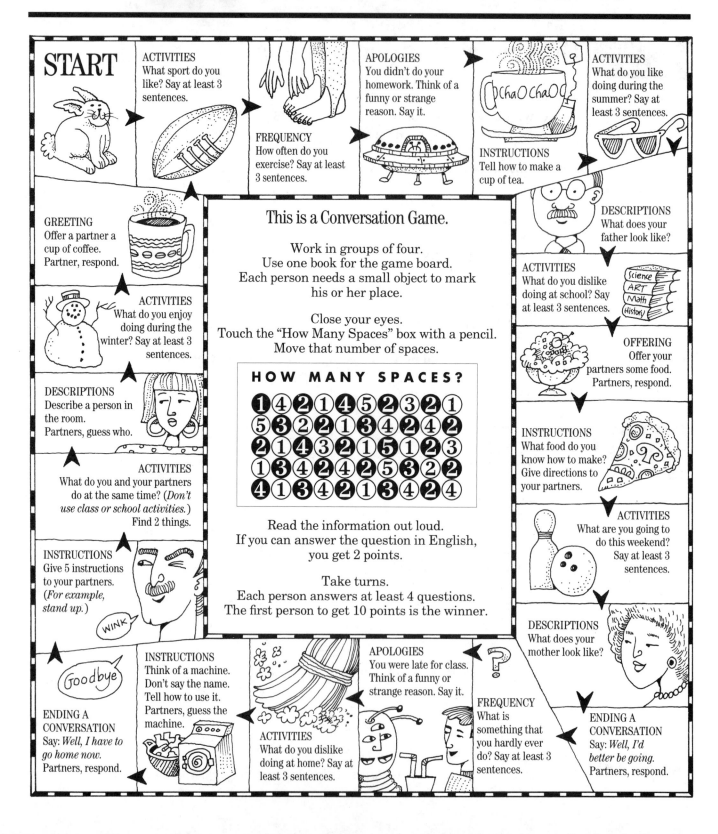

START

ACTIVITIES
What sport do you like? Say at least 3 sentences.

FREQUENCY
How often do you exercise? Say at least 3 sentences.

APOLOGIES
You didn't do your homework. Think of a funny or strange reason. Say it.

INSTRUCTIONS
Tell how to make a cup of tea.

ACTIVITIES
What do you like doing during the summer? Say at least 3 sentences.

DESCRIPTIONS
What does your father look like?

GREETING
Offer a partner a cup of coffee. Partner, respond.

ACTIVITIES
What do you enjoy doing during the winter? Say at least 3 sentences.

DESCRIPTIONS
Describe a person in the room. Partners, guess who.

ACTIVITIES
What do you and your partners do at the same time? (*Don't use class or school activities.*) Find 2 things.

INSTRUCTIONS
Give 5 instructions to your partners. (*For example, stand up.*)

WINK

Goodbye

ENDING A CONVERSATION
Say: *Well, I have to go home now.* Partners, respond.

INSTRUCTIONS
Think of a machine. Don't say the name. Tell how to use it. Partners, guess the machine.

ACTIVITIES
What do you dislike doing at home? Say at least 3 sentences.

APOLOGIES
You were late for class. Think of a funny or strange reason. Say it.

FREQUENCY
What is something that you hardly ever do? Say at least 3 sentences.

ENDING A CONVERSATION
Say: *Well, I'd better be going.* Partners, respond.

DESCRIPTIONS
What does your mother look like?

ACTIVITIES
What are you going to do this weekend? Say at least 3 sentences.

INSTRUCTIONS
What food do you know how to make? Give directions to your partners.

OFFERING
Offer your partners some food. Partners, respond.

Science
ART
Math
History

ACTIVITIES
What do you dislike doing at school? Say at least 3 sentences.

This is a Conversation Game.

Work in groups of four.
Use one book for the game board.
Each person needs a small object to mark his or her place.

Close your eyes.
Touch the "How Many Spaces" box with a pencil.
Move that number of spaces.

HOW MANY SPACES?

1 4 2 1 4 5 2 3 2 1
5 3 2 2 1 3 4 2 4 2
2 1 4 3 2 1 5 1 2 3
1 3 4 2 4 2 5 3 2 2
4 1 3 4 2 1 3 4 2 4

Read the information out loud.
If you can answer the question in English, you get 2 points.

Take turns.
Each person answers at least 4 questions.
The first person to get 10 points is the winner.

Classroom Notes

Note to Teachers:

If you think your students should not see these teaching notes or tape scripts, please ask the students to remove these pages and give them to you.

Procedures for Classroom Teaching

The following suggested procedures and hints can help you use each section of *Talking Together* more effectively. These suggestions are followed with unit-by-unit notes and scripts.

Pronunciation

Talking Together includes two types of *Pronunciation* exercises. In units 1 and 2, the emphasis is on the stress and timing of phrases and syllables. In other units (3, 10, 12, and 14) the emphasis is on the pronunciation of vocabulary used in the unit.

Pronunciation procedure:
- Have the students look at the *Pronunciation* exercise.
- Play the tape or say the words/phrase. Students listen.
- Pause about 2 seconds before having the students repeat. This gives them time to think about what they heard.
- Cue the students to answer with a hand gesture.

As a review at the end of class, have the students close their books and see how many of the words and phrases they remember.

Choice

These are activities in which two answers are given. Students listen and decide which is correct. The procedure is similar to that for the Pronunciation exercises.

Choice procedure:
- Have the students look at the *Choice* exercise.
- Play the tape or say the first words/phrase. Students listen.
- Pause about 2 seconds before having the students repeat. This gives them time to think about what they heard.
- Cue the students to answer with a hand gesture.
- Continue with the rest of the items.

Focus

Focus activities are task-based listening exercises in which the students listen for and write specific information.

In the earlier units, the *Focus* exercises are dictations in which the students write specifically what they hear. However, unlike traditional dictations, students are taught to listen and to **pick out the information they need.**

Later in the book, the *Focus* exercises involve the students' own lives. For example, students are given parts of sentences which they complete with information about themselves.

Focus procedure:
- Have the students look at the *Focus* exercise.
- Read the directions (or play the tape).
- Read the first item from the script in the teacher's notes. Normally you will want to read it twice.
- Allow time for students to think and write between each item.
- Continue until you have read all the items (or played the entire exercise on the tape).
- Correct by assigning students to write one item each on the chalkboard. Other students check to make sure the items are correct. Another way to correct is to have the entire group read the answers as you or another student writes them on the board.

Note that in Units 1, 14, and 15, the students ask you the questions before you say each item. Hold your book so they can see the page, point to the first question and give a hand gesture to cue them to ask it.

Conversation Guide

This section presents short models of interaction.

Conversation Guide procedure:
- Have the students look at the *Conversation Guide.*
- Play the tape or read the conversation to them. Students listen.
- Answer questions about vocabulary, if any.
- Play the "practice" section of the tape or read the conversation again, one line at a time. Students repeat each line.
- Students practice the conversation in pairs. They should practice each part several times. As they practice, circulate and help any pairs that are having difficulty.
- Once students are familiar with a dialogue, they should try to modify it by changing specific information in the conversation.

If students have difficulty with a long sentence during this practice (step 4, above), try "backward build-up." Have them repeat the sentence a phrase at a time. For example (from Unit 8): *Target sentence:* It's between the movie theater and the video shop.

Backward Build-up:
Teacher: the video shop.
Students: the video shop.
Teacher: the movie theater and the video shop.
Students: the movie theater and the video shop.
Teacher: It's between the movie theater and the video shop.
Students: It's between the movie theater and the video shop.

If your students need even more support, write the whole sentence on the board. After the students say the sentence, erase one word, have the students say the sentence, then erase one more word, etc.

Having the students stand and **face each other** while practicing in pairs increases the teacher's class control. You can see what everyone is doing. It is also easy for students to stay interested in the activity since they are more physically involved in it.

As students practice in pairs, encourage **eye contact**. It is standard in English conversation, and it means students are looking away from the book. That helps them remember the conversation. To encourage eye contact, have students stand and face their partners. Tell them to hold their books with one hand. Whenever they speak, they should **put their books by their sides**. They can look back as often as necessary.

For variety and to encourage eye contact (or if you have an odd number of students so they cannot all work in pairs), you may want to have students work in groups of three. Two play the parts of "A" and "B." They close their books. The third person, "C," is the only one with a book open. "C" whispers each line to the speaker, who says it to the partner. "C" may repeat lines as often as necessary.

Group Response

The *Group Response* activities are oral drills. Unlike traditional drills, however, they require decision–making, a step which ensures understanding and builds motivation. These drills allow the students to get over the physical difficulty of saying something in English for the first time. They can also build familiarity and confidence so each student is able to move on to more open situations.

Group Response procedure:
• Have the students look at the *Group Response*.
• Read the directions (or play the tape).
• Read the first question from the script in the teacher's notes. Normally you will want to read the question twice.
• Allow 2 or 3 seconds for students to think. Then cue them to answer with a hand gesture.
• After students have answered, repeat the correct answer so they can make sure they were correct.
• If some of your students do not participate, you may repeat the exercise, this time calling on particular groups or rows of students to answer different items.
• Continue with the rest of the questions.

Some teachers prefer to do the *Group Response* activities twice. The first time the students listen and decide on their answers. The second time they respond more quickly. Generally, students should all respond together rather than being called on individually. This gives all students more practice and avoids embarrassing students who happen to make a mistake.

Hint Boxes

"Hint Boxes" such as this one appear throughout the book.

HINT ☞	**If you don't understand, ask.**
	Could you repeat that?
	What does .... mean?
	How do you spell that?

These boxes contain grammar and usage notes and also clarification phrases. When students don't understand something, encourage them to use the phrases in the hint boxes. Do this by pointing to the phrase in the box and gesturing for them to ask. Getting students to use English to understand what they hear helps them take more responsibility for their own learning.

Using the Classroom Cassette

All of the exercises on the first two pages of each unit are on the Classroom Cassette. Some teachers may prefer to read some or all of the exercises themselves. This is particularly true of the Focus and Group Response activities. The scripts are included in the unit–by–unit Classroom Notes. The scripts are italicized.

On exercises when you are using the tapes, be sure to watch the students. If they have difficulty with an item, you'll want to stop the tape and go back. If the recording for an exercise is too difficult for your students, try reading the script. It is usually easier to understand something spoken in person than from the tape. If it still is too difficult, tell them the answer or have them work in pairs and share their answers. Then play the tape (or read the script) again so they can confirm their answers.

On exercises you choose to read yourself, try not to slow down. It doesn't help students if they learn to understand only unnaturally slow, perfectly enunciated English. Don't read slowly, word-by-word. Instead read naturally (in groups of words), but leave longer pauses at the breaks between word groups and sentences. This gives students time to think.

Pair Practice

As indicated in the introduction, *Pair Practice* is a highly effective and motivating way for students to learn English. The activities in *Talking Together* are based on the idea of students using English to "cross an information gap." That is, one partner (A) knows something that the other (B) doesn't. B needs to get the information to complete the task.

It is important that students **never look at their partner's book** during the task. If they do, it destroys the purpose of the activity and eliminates the interest.

Front of Classroom

Figure 1   Figure 2   **77**

Pair Practice procedure:

• Divide the class into pairs. Half the students are A. The other half are B.

• A's look at the A page in their books. B's look at the B page.

• Select one pair that everyone can see. Demonstrate the task by directing that pair through the first few steps while the other students watch.

• When most students understand the task, tell all the pairs to begin.

• As students work, walk around the room. Help and encourage students who are having difficulty. Listen for mistakes and note them for later work (see "corrections," below).

• As pairs finish the main tasks, tell them to go on to the *Just for Fun* mini-task at the bottom of the page.

Special hints for Pair Practice

Dividing the class into pairs. It is best if students can face their partners. Do this by having all the students in odd numbered seats (1st, 3rd, 5th, etc.) in each row be A. The A's turn around in their chairs. They don't need to move their desks. See Figure 1, above.

Have students work with the person behind/in front of themselves. It eliminates the problem of students copying from each other's book since it is almost impossible for them to read upside-down.

Giving instructions. It is always better to demonstrate what to do rather than explaining it. Demonstration avoids confusing students the way explanations (either in English or in their native language) can. Demonstrate by having one pair serve as the model. Direct those students through the first few steps. The other students will quickly understand. The instructions in *Talking Together* are short and written in simple language. When you read the instructions more than once, use the same words. This makes it easier for the students to know what to do.

Introducing Pair Practice for the first time. If your students are not accustomed to pair practice, you may want to do the first *Pair Practice* as a full group activity. You take the part of A. All of the students are B. Ask specific students for answers. Prompt them to ask you the questions from their page. After most of the students understand the idea, put them in pairs and have them do the exercises with a partner. If there are a few students who still don't understand, you can work with them individually because most of the students will be working independently.

Encouraging students to use English only. It is important that students understand the purpose of pair work. Remind them pair work is really a kind of drill. It gives students practice in actually using English. It helps them learn it both for tests and for actual use.

If you find your students start to use their native languages too much during the activity, try this technique: Have each student take out a piece of paper. They make a mark on the paper every time they say anything in English. At the end, check to see which students have the most marks. This technique puts the responsibility of using English on the students. It is more effective than continuous reminders from the teacher to use English only.

Students work at different speeds. Because students are really communicating, they won't all work at the same speed. Naturally, some students finish before others. Those students should go on to the *Just for Fun* mini-task which appears at the bottom of the pair work page. These instructions are easy to understand so they don't need to be explained. Because stronger students go on to this activity, it gives weaker students time to finish the main task.

Correcting mistakes. Some teachers worry that students working in pairs will be "practicing mistakes." This shouldn't be a concern for two major reasons. First, the students have had, during the preparation activities, enough practice with similar tasks so there won't be too many mistakes. Secondly, as teachers we need to remember (and help students understand) that *mistakes are not bad*. They are a natural part of the learning process. There will be a few more mistakes than in a traditional classroom class where only one student speaks at a time. Remember, there is also hundreds of times more correct practice going on, too!

There are times, of course, when we want to provide feedback to make students aware of their mistakes. Corrections are always more effective if the students, rather than the teacher, are able to come up with the correct forms. The following techniques are ways to help students correct their own mistakes:

• As students do the *Pair Practice*, walk around the room and listen for the kinds of mistakes people are making. Write six or eight sentences containing the mistakes on the chalkboard. Have the students tell you how to correct them.

• Correct forms are always presented in the book, either on the *Pair Practice* pages or in the preparation activities. As you circulate, when you hear a mistake that is interfering with understanding, silently point to the correct form in the student's book and encourage the student to correct the sentence.

• Finger signals are a very effective way to help students do their own corrections. When you hear a mistake, ask the student to repeat the sentence. You point to one finger for each word. See Figure 2, above.

Then point to the part of the sentence containing the mistake. You can use other gestures to indicate that the student needs to add a word or ending, remove a word, change word order, etc. Just think of each finger as representing one word. Any gesture that gives the student a hint will be useful.

UNIT NOTES

The step-by-step procedures for each section of *Talking Together* are outlined in the previous pages. The following are hints for teaching each particular unit, tape scripts, usage notes, vocabulary lists, and warm-up/expansion activities.

UNIT 1: Personal Information

Note: See pages 75–77 for teaching procedures, strategies, and hints. All activities except the Pair Practice are on the cassette.

PRONUNCIATION
Listen. Repeat.
What's your **name**?   My name's **Mari**. I'm **Mari**.
Where do you **live**?   In **Osaka**.
What do you **do**?   I'm a **student**.
What do you **do** in your **free time**?   I **listen** to **music**.
                                        I like **jazz**.
• The words in **bold** are stressed. As students listen and repeat, use hand gestures to emphasize the stress.
• Note that contracted forms ("I'm" for "I am", "name's" for "name is") are used. These are standard in spoken English and informal written English.

FOCUS
 The students ask the questions.
Ask questions about this woman. Listen. Write the answers.
1. {*Mary.*}
2. {*In Florida.*}
3. {*She's a businesswoman.*}
4. {*Listen to music.*}
Listen. Write the information.
This is {Mike}.
He lives in {Toronto, Canada}.
He is a {student}.
He likes {swimming}.
• Correct by having students read the information to you or by having individual students write the answers on the chalkboard.

CONVERSATION GUIDE
Listen.
1.   *A: Where does Ms. Lima live?*
       B: Excuse me?
     A: Where does she live?
       B: In San Francisco.
2.   *A: What does Mr. Williams do?*
       B: He's a teacher.
     A: What does he do in his free time?
       B: He likes watching movies.
Practice the conversations.

• Some students may refer to free time activities and interests as "hobbies." In American English, hobbies usually refer to activities done by children. They can also be used for interests such as collecting things (stamps, coins, etc.). "Free time activities" and "interests" generally sound more adult.

GROUP RESPONSE
• As you ask the questions, you may want to hold your book so the students can see the page. Wait one or two seconds after asking, then point to the area containing the answer. Gesture for students to respond.
Look at the chart. Listen and answer the questions.
1. *Where does Ms. Lima live?*   {*She lives in San Francisco.*}
2. *What does Mr. Williams do?*   {*He's a teacher.*}
3. *Where does Mr. Choy live?*   {*He lives in Seoul*}
4. *What does Ms. Ito do?*   {*She's a taxi driver.*}
5. *What does Ms. Lima do?*   {*She's a lawyer.*}
6. *What does Ms. Lima do in her free time?*
                               {*She likes driving.*}
7. *What does Mr. Choy do in his free time?*
                          {*He likes listening to music.*}
8. *Where does Ms. Ito live?*   {*She lives in Honolulu.*}
9. *What does Mr. Williams do in his free time?*
                           {*He likes watching movies.*}
10. *What does Mr. Choy do?*   {*He's a student.*}
Now listen again and check your answers.

PAIR PRACTICE
• See page 77 for the suggestions about giving instructions.
• If your students aren't used to doing pair work, have them work through the activity with you playing the part of A. The students are B. Then have them repeat it in pairs.
• Students may give short answers rather than full forms (example: A: "Where does Jim live?" B: Miami. rather than "He lives in Miami.") This is acceptable. However, if you want them to practice the full forms, tell them.
• Write "When you finish, do 'Just for Fun!'" on the chalkboard. As pairs finish, point to the board and indicate that they should continue. Don't explain the activity. You want them to get in the habit of going on to these tasks without waiting for your instructions. The instructions are simple enough for most students to understand.
• Questions people ask each other when they meet vary between cultures. In most English-speaking countries, one does not ask about age, salary, religion, or politics. These topics are considered personal.

UNIT 1: ACTIVE VOCABULARY

designer	lawyer	student	pilot (retired)
taxi driver	teacher	camp	dance
drive	hike	free time activity	
spell	swim	repeat	
listen (to music)		watch (movies)	

WARM–UP/EXPANSION ACTIVITIES

• **Names on Their Backs.** Prepare pieces of paper with the names of famous people—one name for each student. (You can use some names more than once.) Tape one name to each student's back. Students stand and walk around the room. They ask questions (Am I a man or a woman? Where am I from? What do I do? etc.). They try to guess the name. Variation: Give one name to each student. They can look at it. Partners ask the question and try to guess the name. Categories: actors, politicians, athletes, business people, writers, scientists, musicians.

• **Who is it?** Students each write four sentences about themselves. Separate the sentences and mix them up. Give one to each student. They must stand and circulate. They ask questions to find out who wrote their sentence. When they find someone, they get another sentence from you. The winner is the person who finds the most.

UNIT 2: Numbers

Note: See pages 75–77 for teaching procedures, strategies, and hints. All activities except the pair practice are on the cassette.

Many students will already know the numbers in English. Most students, however, have a difficult time actually using them, especially when they are spoken rapidly. Encourage the learners to work on speed during this unit.

FOCUS

• Read each item two times.
Listen. Write the numbers.

a. {20}   b. {14}   c. {93}   d. {17}   e. {84}

f. {44} students   g. {12} teachers   h. {73} people
i. {21} Americans   j. {36} children

k. There are {42} men and {57} women.
l. I have {18} books and {26} magazines.
m. {27} students and {14} teachers went to the meeting.
n. There are {11} buildings and {98} rooms.
o. There are {15} Japanese, {18} Koreans and {23} Chinese in the class.

• Correct by having the students read the numbers to you. Write them on the chalkboard.

PRONUNCIATION

• Use short and long hand gestures to help the students notice the difference in syllable length.
• In American English the "ty" in 20 is usually pronounced with a silent "t" /tweny/. In other numbers (30, 40, etc.) it is pronounced almost like a /d/: /thirdy/.

Listen.

a. (13) *thirteen*   (30) *thirty*   f. (22) *twenty-two*

b. (14) *fourteen*   (40) *forty*   g. (47) *forty-seven*

c. (16) *sixteen*   (60) *sixty*   h. (66) *sixty-six*

d. (17) *seventeen* (70) *seventy*   i. (79) *seventy-nine*

e. (19) *nineteen*   (90) *ninety*   j. (86) *eighty-six*

Now listen and say the numbers.   k. (91) *ninety-one*

CHOICE

• Read each item two times.
Circle the number you hear.

a. {15}   b. {90}   c. {40}
d. {17} students
e. {30} countries
f. {12} books
g. There are {88} cards.
h. I have {50} dollars
i. There are {16} tickets.
j. He was born {37} years ago.

• Correct by having the students read the numbers to you. Write them on the chalkboard.

CONVERSATION GUIDE

• After they've practiced the conversation, have the students continue. They should talk about things they have (books, brothers and sisters, etc.)
Listen.
1. A: How many tickets do you have?
        B: I have FIFTEEN.
    A: What did you say?
        B: FIFTEEN.
    A: Thanks.
2. A: How many students are in your class?
        B : There are FIFty
    A: Did you say "FIFTEEN" or "FIFty"?
        B: I said, "FIFty."
    A: Fifty? Thanks.
Practice the conversations.

PAIR PRACTICE

• Note the suggestions for giving instructions on page 77.
• Write "When you finish, do 'Just for Fun!'" on the chalkboard. As pairs finish, point to the board and indicate that they should continue. Don't explain the activity. You want them to get in the habit of going on to these tasks without waiting for your instructions. The instructions are simple enough for most students to understand.

UNIT 2: ACTIVE VOCABULARY

Chinese	Japanese	Korean
bottle	CDs (compact discs)	
flower	glass	magazine
people	pizza	plate
poster	sandwich	tickets
TVs	video tape	

WARM–UP/EXPANSION ACTIVITIES

• **Tap the Numbers.** Students work in groups of four or five. One thinks of a number between 10 and 99. That student taps on the desk to indicate the number. Tap for each numeral ("37" is 3 taps, then 7 taps. Don't tap 37 times). Partners try to be the first to say the number. The person who is first thinks of another number and taps it. They continue.

• **Telephone Directory.** Students work in groups of about ten. They make a list of all the people in their group. Then, working in pairs, they ask for and write their partner's phone number. They then change partners and find out someone else's number. They continue until they have everyone's number. Variation: Give the students a time limit (5-8 minutes). They circulate and get as many numbers as possible in that time.

• **BUZZ.** Go around the class, counting to 100. Each student says one number. The rule: Don't say any number with a 3 in it (13, 23, 31, etc.). Also don't say any number that you can divide by 3 (3, 6, 9, etc.). Instead, say, "Buzz." Example: One. Two. Buzz. Four. Five. Buzz. Seven... Try it again. This time, leave out 7's.

UNIT 3: The Time

Note: See pages 75–77 for teaching procedures, strategies, and hints. All activities except the pair practice are on the cassette.

PRONUNCIATION

• Read each item two times.

Look at the clocks. Listen. Repeat the times.

It's one o'clock.

It's one-fifteen.	*(or)*	*It's a quarter past one.*
It's one-thirty.	*(or)*	*It's half past one.*
It's one-forty-five.	*(or)*	*It's a quarter to two.*
It's one-ten.	*(or)*	*It's ten past one.*
It's one-twenty.	*(or)*	*It's twenty past one.*
It's one-forty.	*(or)*	*It's twenty to two.*
It's one-fifty.	*(or)*	*It's ten to two.*

It's twelve o'clock. It's noon. It's midnight.

• "O'clock" is used for hours only. It can't be used if minutes are included.

• "After" can be used instead of "past." "Till" or "of" can be used instead of "to."

GROUP RESPONSE

• Read each question two times.

Look at the bus schedule. Listen to the questions. Say the answers.

• *When does the northbound bus leave San Diego?*
  { 5:30 a.m. }
• *What time does the northbound bus depart Monterey?*
  { 3:30 p.m. }
• *Does the bus arrive in Los Angeles at 8:41 a.m.?*
  { Yes, it does. }
• *When does the bus from San Diego get to Santa Barbara?*
  { 10:44 a.m. }
• *What time does the northbound bus get to San Francisco?*
  { 7 p.m. }

Look at the schedule for the southbound bus, the bus that goes from San Francisco to San Diego.

• *What time does the bus leave San Francisco?*
  { 7 a.m. }
• *When does the bus arrive in Los Angeles?*
  { 6:23 p.m. }
• *What time does the bus leave Monterey?*
  { 12 noon }
• *Does the bus arrive in Santa Barbara before 3 p.m.?*
  { No, it doesn't. }
• *Does the bus arrive in San Diego at 10:30 p.m.?*
  { No, it doesn't. It arrives at 9:30 p.m. }

Now listen again and check your answers.

• For additional practice, have students work in three's. One person asks an additional question. The partners try to be first to answer. The person who answers correctly asks the next question.

• Many countries use a 24-hour clock for bus, train and airplane schedules. In the United States, a 12-hour clock is usually used. If there is a possibility of being misunderstood, "a.m. / p.m. / in the morning / at night," etc. are used.

CONVERSATION GUIDE

Listen.

1. *A: Excuse me. What time is it ?*
   B: It's two o'clock.
   A: Thanks.
   B: You're welcome.
2. *A: Is it three o'clock yet?*
   B: No, it isn't. It's two forty-five.
   A: OK. Thanks.
   B: You're welcome.

Practice the conversations.

• For variety, have students think of situations in which they might ask someone for the time (waiting for a test to start, waiting for a phone call from a boy or girlfriend, waiting for a concert to start, waiting to see the dentist). Write the situations on the chalkboard. As students practice, they imagine themselves in the different situations and change their voices to show their feelings.

FOCUS
• Read each item two times.
Listen. Write the times.
a. I get up at { 7:00.} ...at seven o'clock.
b. We leave school at { 3:30.} ...at half past three.
c. I have an appointment at { 9:20.} ...twenty after nine.
d. The movie starts at { 7:50.} ...ten to eight.
e. I usually eat lunch at { 12:00.} ...at twelve o'clock.
f. I usually go to bed at { 11:15.} ...at quarter after eleven.
g. I leave work every day at { 4:45.} ...at quarter to five.
h. When do you leave home in the morning? At { 8:10.}
i. When is your English class? It starts at { 1:20.} At 1:20?
    That's right.
j. When does the bus leave? It leaves at { 8:38.}
    You'd better hurry.

PAIR PRACTICE
• Students usually need more practice with phrases such as "a quarter after..." and "half-past." Encourage them to use these forms.
• Steps 3 and 4 work best if students use available materials. They can use a pencil or pen to represent the minute hand of a clock and a short pencil for the hour hand.

UNIT 3: ACTIVE VOCABULARY

noon	midnight	half	quarter
catch	cook	get up	guess
have	pantomime	read	study
breakfast	dinner	lunch	art
biology	chemistry	English	geography
history	math	physics	physical education

WARM–UP/EXPANSION ACTIVITIES
• **Every 15 Minutes.** Students work in groups of four. One person starts by saying what time he or she usually gets up on Sunday. (I get up at 8:00). The next person says what he or she is doing fifteen minutes later (I read the newspaper at 8:15). They continue in fifteen-minute segments. The group that gets the furthest through the day in the time allowed is the winner.
• **Guess What Time.** As a full group, think of activities most people do every weekend. Write the list on the chalkboard. Also write: I think you ....(ed) at .... : .... . Students then stand and circulate. They each find a partner and try to guess what time the partner did one of the activities. The partner cannot speak. He or she can only nod "yes" or point up or down to mean "later" or "earlier." After each correct guess, they change partners.

UNIT 4: Dates

Note: See pages 75–77 for teaching procedures, strategies, and hints. All activities except the pair practice are on the cassette.

FOCUS
• Read each item two times.
• Don't slow down or overemphasize the dates in sentences 6–10. If students have difficulty, read the sentences at normal speed but pause longer than usual at natural breaks.
Listen. Write only the dates. Don't write the sentences.
1. {April 18, 1906}
2. {July 14, 1977}
3. {May 7, 1987}
4. {January 23, 1974}
5. {November 15}
6. {April 12, 1961} is the day the first person flew in space.
7. {October 10th} is a holiday in Taiwan.
    It's called Double Tens.
8. Christmas is {December 25.}
9. She was born {September 1, 1970.}
10. {February 14} is a special day. It's Valentine's Day.

CHOICE
• Read the sentences. Give them time to think before they repeat.
Listen. Repeat the sentences. Circle on or in.
1. New Year's is {in} January.
2. Ms. Park's birthday is {in} July.
3. Janet was born {on} December 10, 1972.
4. School begins on Monday and finishes {on} Friday.
5. They went to Taiwan {in} 1991.
6. I graduated from university {in} June, 1990.
• Some students have difficulty hearing the difference between "in" and "on." If so, write the words on the chalkboard and have students point to the one they say in each sentence.

CONVERSATION GUIDE
Listen.
1. A: Pardon me. What's the date today?
        B: It's Monday, the 18th.
    A: The 18th?
        B: Yes.
2. A: Excuse me. When's the science test?
        B: It's on the 23rd.
    A: The 23rd?
        B: That's right.
3. A: Pardon me. When were the Barcelona Olympics?
        B: They were in 1992.
    A: 1992? Thanks.
        B: Sure.
Practice the conversations.
• Note that ordinal numbers (1st , 2nd, etc.) are usually used for dates.

GROUP RESPONSE

• Some of the questions are worded a little differently than what is written on the calender (example: The calendar says "exam" but the question says "test."). This is to make sure the students think about their answers.

Look at the calendar. Listen to the questions. Say the answers.

1. *When's Bill's test?*	*{July 7th}*
2. *When's the next Giants baseball game?*	*{July 5th}*
3. *When's American Independence Day?*	*{July 4th}*
4. *When's his sister's birthday?*	*{July 29th}*
5. *When's his lunch with his co-worker?*	*{July 8th}*
6. *When's the Whitney Houston concert?*	*{July 11th}*
7. *When does he start vacation?*	*{July 12th}*
8. *When does he go back to work?*	*{July 21st}*
9. *When is his last history class?*	*{July 10th}*
10. *When is the barbecue?*	*{July 3rd}*

Now listen again and check your answers.

PAIR PRACTICE

• Parts 3 and 4 should take on a game-like feeling. There is no reason the students should know the answers in advance. How many guesses it takes is primarily luck. Remember, wrong answers provide extra practice. You may want the students to count how many questions they ask. The "winner" is the person who asks the fewest.

UNIT 4: ACTIVE VOCABULARY

concert	die	election	finish
game	invent	join	open
party	start	visit	

WARM–UP/EXPANSION ACTIVITIES

• **Birthday Fruit Basket.** (This is a large class activity.) You need one less chair than the number of students. The student who is standing calls out a month. All students whose birthdays are in that month change seats. The standing student tries to get one of the seats. Whoever is left standing calls out a different month. The game continues. Once students understand the rules, have them do it with dates. The standing student calls out 3 dates (the 10th, the 23rd, the 2nd.) Students whose birthdays are on those dates— in any month—change seats.

• **Line Up.** Work in groups of about 10 students. Ask each other their birthdays. Make a line. The person with the first birthday of the year is 1st. The second birthday is next. When you finish, think of other ways to make lines. Example: How long have you lived in this town? How old are you?

• **Writing in the Air.** Each student thinks of an important date. It can be a time in history or something personal. Students stand and circulate. They work in pairs. With their fingers, they "write" the date in the air. Their partner must say the date and guess the meaning. They then change partners and continue.

UNIT 5: Names and Addresses

Note: See pages 75–77 for teaching procedures, strategies, and hints. All activities except the Pair Practice are on the cassette.

GROUP RESPONSE

Put the addresses in order. Number the lines. Say the addresses. Now listen and check your answers.

Ms. Maria Moss	*Mr. Y. S. Kim*
8619 N. 14th Ave.	*89135 N. Pacific Blvd.*
Tampa, Florida	*San Diego, California*
33610	*92101*

• The order in the students books is as follows:

{4}	{3}
{2}	{1}
{1}	{4}
{3}	{2}

• Numbers in addresses are usually read alone or in groups of two: 8619 could be "eight six one nine" or "eighty-six nineteen." It isn't read "Eight thousand six hundred nineteen."

• "O" (zero) is *sometimes* pronounced /oh/ in addresses and telephone numbers.

• Ms. (pronounced "miz") is becoming common as an address form for adult women. "Miss" and "Mrs." (pronounced "missuz") are still commonly used.

FOCUS: Spelling

• Pauses are shown with this symbol: //.
If you are using the tape, press the pause or stop button.

• Prompt the students to ask you how to spell each item after you say it. Do this by gesturing or by pointing to the "Hint Box" in the book.

Listen to the names and places. Ask how to spell them. Write them.

1. *{Arizona}* — *// Capital A-r-i-z-o-n-a*
2. *{43 Sixth Street}* — *// Forty-three capital S-i-x-t-h capital S-t-r-e-e-t*
3. *{Barry F. Walker}* — *// Capital B-a-r-r-y capital F period capital W-a-l-k-e-r*
4. *{The Grand Hotel}* — *// Capital T-h-e capital G-r-a-n-d capital H-o-t-e-l*
5. *{735 Queensland Place}* — *// Seven-three-five capital Q-u-e-e-n-s-l-a-n-d capital P-l-a-c-e*
6. *{Yokohama, Japan}* — *// Capital Y-o-k-o-h-a-m-a comma capital J-a-p-a-n*

CONVERSATION GUIDE

Listen.

1. *A: It's at 469 Beale Street.*
   *B: **Did you say** Beale Street?*
   A: Yes, that's right.
2. *A: It's at 469 Beale Street.*
   *B: **Could you repeat that?***
   A: 469 Beale Street.
   B: Thank you.

3. *A: It's at 469 Beale Street.*
   B: **How do you spell** *Beale?*
   A: B-E-A-L-E.
   B: Thank you.

Practice the conversations.
• After the students have practiced, you may want to have them circulate. They use their own address and write their partner's address. Then they change partners and continue.

FOCUS: Prepositions and Abbreviations
Note: Give the students a few minutes to read and write their answers before playing the tape / reading the correct information.

• Read each item two times.
Read the sentences. Write the correct preposition.
1. *He lives {on} Fourth Street.*
2. *They are staying {at} 458 North Spring Road.*
3. *He lives {in} Pusan, Korea.*
4. *She has {an} apartment {on} River Street.*
5. *He used to live {in} Vancouver.*

Many parts of an address have short forms — abbreviations. Write the abbreviations.

street	capital {S-t} period	North	capital {N} period
avenue	capital {A-v-e} period	South	capital {S} period
road	capital {R-d} period	East	capital {E} period
apartment	capital {A-p-t} period	West	capital {W} period
building	capital {B-l-d-g} period		

• To check, you may want the students to read the words to you as you write them on the chalkboard.

PAIR PRACTICE
• Many students will recognize Parts 1 and 2 as the game "hangman." If your students aren't familiar with the game, you may want to teach it by using your city or school name as an example. Write the correct number of lines on the chalkboard. Students guess letters. They try to guess the word. If students are reluctant to guess in front of the class, have everyone stand. Students can sit down once they have guessed whether they were right or wrong.

UNIT 5: ACTIVE VOCABULARY

address	apartment	avenue	building
road	street	postal code	zip code
North	South	East	West
capital	period	comma	

WARM–UP/EXTENSION ACTIVITIES
• **A to Z.** Students work in groups of three or four. Each group needs a sheet of paper. On it they write all the letters, A through Z. One student then spells his or her name. They cross out those letters. The next student continues. After each student has spelled his or her name, the group must think of other words that use the remaining letters. Variation: Instead of spelling names, students think of words. They spell them. They get one point for each letter that has not been crossed out before.
• **Whose Address?** Each student writes his or her address on a piece of paper. Collect the papers, mix them, and redistribute them. Students stand and circulate. Then they ask other students their addresses until they find the person whose address is written on their paper.

REVIEW UNIT: Social Conversation

• The "social conversation" units of *Talking Together* are for a slightly different purpose than the others. The first page of each introduces standard examples of patterns used for common social interaction. The second page is a review game that covers the previous five units.
• The procedures for Conversation Guide and Group Response are the same as for the other units (See pages 75–77).

CONVERSATION GUIDE
Listen.
• Greeting
1. *A: Hi, Emi. How are you doing?*
      B: Pretty good. How about you?
   A: Not bad. How was your weekend?
      B: It was great. I went to a concert.
2. *A: Hello, Kent. How are you?*
      B: Fine, thanks. And you?

• Inviting
3. *A: Would you like to go to a movie Saturday?*
      B: That sounds good.
4. *A: Do you want to go to a concert Friday?*
      B: Sorry, I have to work. Maybe another time.
   A: OK.

• Suggesting
5. *A: How about the new Micky Rourke film?*
      B: Great. I love his movies.
6. *A: Let's go to the jazz concert.*
      B: Well, I don't really like jazz.
         How about something else?
   A: OK.

Practice the conversations.
• Because of the social nature of these conversations, you may want to have students move around the classroom. They do each part with a different partner.
• You may want to ask students what movies are currently playing in your area, what concerts are coming and what restaurants they like to visit. List them on the board. Students use those items as they practice.
• After students have practiced the separate sections, have them try to put them together in a longer conversation.

GROUP RESPONSE
• Give the students a short time to read the choices before you say each line.
Listen. Choose an answer. Circle the letter. Say your answer.
1. *Hi. How are you?*
    c. {Fine, thanks. And you?}
2. *Do you want to go to the beach tomorrow?*
    a. {Sorry, I have to work.}
3. *Let's go dancing tomorrow.*
    b. {Great. I love dancing.}
4. *How was your weekend?*
    c. {Great. I went to a baseball game.}
5. *How are you doing?*
    c. {Pretty good. How about you?}
6. *Would you like to go to a movie Friday?*
    a. {That sounds good.}
7. *Let's go to an Indian restaurant tonight.*
    b. {I don't really like Indian food. How about Chinese?}
8. *How about the New China Cafe?*
    a. {That sounds good.}

THE SMALL TALK GAME
• This is a fluency game. Students should be thinking about meaning rather than form. If you hear grammatical errors, note them but don't correct immediately. (See page 77 for more information on corrections.)
• Be sure students continue playing until each has answered at least four questions. Don't worry if different players land on the same question. Their answers will be different.
• If a student lands on a question he or she has already answered, that student should answer it again using different information. Another option is to make a rule that when a student lands on a question a second time, any partner can ask any question (a different one from the game or one the partner thinks of).
• If dice are available, you may want to use them instead of the "How Many Spaces" box.

UNIT 6: Large Numbers

Note: See pages 75–77 for teaching procedures, strategies, and hints. All activities except the pair practice are on the cassette.

FOCUS: Vocabulary
• You may want to preview this activity by writing a large number on the chalkboard. Have the students read it together. Then erase the number one numeral at a time. Students read the remaining number.
• Read each number two times.
Write the words. Then write the numbers.
a. *Two {million}, four {hundred} thirty-two {thousand}, nine {hundred} twenty-one. {2,432,921}*

b. *Thirty-two {million}, seventy-four {thousand}, one. {32,074,001}*
c. *Three {million}, sixty-seven {thousand}, seven {hundred} twelve. {3,067,712}*
• Correct by having individual students write their answers on the chalkboard or by having the class dictate the numbers to you as you write them on the board.

FOCUS: Large Numbers
• Don't slow down or overemphasize the numbers in sentences 6–10. If students have difficulty, read the sentences at normal speed but pause longer than usual at natural breaks.
• Read each item two times.
Write the numbers. Don't write the sentences.
1. *Two hundred thirteen {213}*
2. *Eight hundred sixteen {816}*
3. *One thousand ninety-one {1,091}*
4. *Five thousand, one hundred, eleven {5,111}*
5. *Nine thousand, nine hundred seventeen {9,917}*
6. *There are ten thousand, two hundred seventeen students at the university. {10, 217}*
7. *The population is one hundred forty-six thousand, nine hundred. {146,900}*
8. *One million, one hundred twenty-six thousand, nine hundred eighteen people visited Disneyland last year. {1,126,918}*
9. *The building cost twenty-three million, two hundred fourteen thousand, seven hundred nineteen dollars. {23,214,719}*
10. *The answer is nine hundred forty-six million, three hundred twenty-one thousand, five hundred eighty-seven. {946,321,587}*

CONVERSATION GUIDE
Listen.
1. *A: What's the population of Australia?*
    B: Could you repeat that?
    A: What is the population of Australia?
    B: It's 16,500,000.
2. *A: What's the population of Singapore?*
    B: It's 2,600,000.
    A: Did you say 2,060,000?
    B: No. 2,600,000.
Practice the conversations.
• If students don't know the meaning of "population," explain by using the population of their city or country as an example.
• Once students have practiced the conversations, they can change them using the information on the chart in Group Response.

GROUP RESPONSE
• Ask each question twice. After you ask, give the students a few seconds to think before gesturing for them to answer.

Look at the chart. Listen to the questions. Say the answers.
1. *What is the population of Brazil?* {119,098,992}
2. *What is the population of the U.S.?* {226,594,725}
3. *What is the population of Singapore?* {2,600,000}
4. *What is the population of the United Kingdom?* {57,100,000}
5. *What is the population of Japan?* {117,057,485}
6. *What is the population of Australia?* {16,500,000}

PAIR PRACTICE
• Students will be familiar with the first activity since it is very similar to the Group Response on the previous page.
• Make sure students understand that Step 2 is a guessing game. There is no reason students should know the answers beforehand.

UNIT 6: ACTIVE VOCABULARY

hundred	thousand	million	area
population	square kilometers (sq. km.)		about
almost	nearly	over	island

WARM–UP/EXPANSION ACTIVITIES
• **My Numbers.** Students each write down five large numbers that are important to them. They can be dates, club membership numbers, credit card numbers, etc. They should not be "secret numbers" (bank cards, etc.). They then dictate the numbers to a partner who writes them and guesses the meaning. Then they change partners.
• **Tap the Numbers II.** Repeat the expansion activity from Unit 2 using numbers between 10,000 and 999,999,999. Students work in groups of four or five. One thinks of a number. That student taps on the desk to indicate the number. Tap for each numeral ("42, 215" is 4 taps, 2 taps, 2 taps, 1 tap and 5 taps). Partners try to be the first to say the number. The person who is first thinks of another number and taps it. They continue.

UNIT 7: Definitions
....

Note: See pages 75–77 for teaching procedures, strategies, and hints. All activities except the pair practice are on the cassette.

FOCUS: Matching
• Give the students one or two minutes before reading the sentences. Students try to answer on their own.
• Have students tell you the extra items they wrote for the first part. You may want to do the same activity with the groups listed in the matching exercise.
• Say each sentence two times.
Look at the groups. Can you find two more examples for each group? Match the words to their groups. Listen and check.
A sweater is a type of {clothing}. A lion is a kind of {animal}. A hammer is a kind of {tool}.   A chair is a type of {furniture}. Pizza is a kind of {food}.

• Check by having the students read their sentences back to you.

FOCUS: Definitions
• You may want to let the students fill in the blanks before they listen. Then they can see if their answers were the same.
• Encourage students to ask about words they don't understand. Do this by pointing to "What does ... mean?" in the Hint Box. Since most students will be familiar with the items, it is easy to help them understand the meaning of new words.
• Read each sentence two times.
What is it made from? Listen. Write the words.
1. *Furniture is usually made from {wood, metal, or plastic}.*
2. *Pizza is made from {flour, water, vegetables, meat, and cheese}.*
3. *Books are made from {paper}.*
4. *The warmest sweaters are made from {wool}.*

CONVERSATION GUIDE
Listen.
1. *A: What's lasagne?*
   B: It's a food. It's made from pasta, meat, and cheese.
2. *A: What's that?*
   B: It's a modem.
   A: A modem?
   B: Yes. I use it for sending computer messages.
3. *A: What's that?*
   B: It's a llama.
   A: A llama?
   B: Yes, they live in South America.
Practice the conversations.
• Students may not be familiar with the items (lasagne, a modem, a llama). That is intentional. It puts them in a situation of asking for information about things they don't know.
• If you have objects (or pictures of things) from other cultures that students aren't familiar with, have them continue practicing using those items.

GROUP RESPONSE
• Wait 2–3 seconds after reading the sentences before gesturing for a response. This gives all the students a chance to think.
Listen. Which things are they talking about? Say the answers. Number the pictures (1–7).
1. *You use it to cut wood.*
   This is used for cutting wood. {a saw}
2. *It's used to tell time.*
   You can use this for telling time. {a watch}
3. *It's for sending information.*
   Use this machine to send information. {a fax machine}
4. *You can use one of these to move things quickly.*
   It's for moving things. {a truck}

5. *This is used for writing and doing mathematics.*
    You can use it to write and to do math. {a <u>computer</u>}
6. *This is for buying things.*
    You can use one when you buy something. {a <u>credit card</u>}
7. *This is for keeping things cold.*
    It will keep things cold. {a <u>fridge</u> [<u>refrigerator</u>]}

Listen. What is being described?
8. *It's a long musical instrument. It's made of wood. It has six strings. There's a sound box behind the strings. Some are electric.* {<u>guitar</u>}
9. *This is a kind of game. It's played on a green table. There are six holes in the table. A long stick, called a cue, is used to hit balls into the holes.* {<u>billiards</u> or <u>pool</u>}
10. *These are used for eating. They are most common in Asian countries like Japan, China, and a few others. They are long sticks made of wood or plastic.* {<u>chopsticks</u>}

PAIR PRACTICE
• This activity works best if it takes on a game-like feeling.

UNIT 7: ACTIVE VOCABULARY

animal	clothing	saw	tool	cloth	crust
flour	fur	leather	metal	plastic	round
spices	hammer	llama	modem	furniture	
fax (facsimile) machine			refrigerator (fridge)		

WARM–UP/EXPANSION ACTIVITIES
• **What is it?** Students work in groups of about five. One student thinks of an object. That student begins to draw a picture of the object one line at a time. After each line, the student gives a hint (It's made of .... I use it to .... etc.). Partners try to guess the object before the picture is complete.
• **Do it Yourself – Find the Mistakes.** Use this activity after students have done the Pair Practice in this unit. Students work in pairs. Each thinks of an object and describes it, including several mistakes (as they did during the Pair Practice). Partners listen and try to find the mistakes.

UNIT 8: Locations and Directions

Note: See pages 75–77 for teaching procedures, strategies, and hints. All activities except the pair practice are on the cassette.

PRONUNCIATION
Listen. Repeat the phrases.

Turn right.	*It's around the corner from*
Turn left.	*the bank.*
Go straight.	*It's between two houses.*
It's on the corner.	*It's on the left of the house.*
It's in the middle of the street.	*It's next to a house.*
It's across from the house.	*It's on the right of the house.*

• Use hand gestures to indicate the meaning. Encourage the students to gesture as they speak.
• After they have done the activity, you may want students to work in pairs. One partner closes the book. The other gestures the words. The first partner says them.

FOCUS
• Most of the sentences in this activity and the rest of the unit use "landmarks" (well-known places) instead of street names. This is a useful strategy for students in countries where not all streets have names. It is also useful for visitors who can often find landmarks more easily than specific streets.
Look at the pictures. Can you write the words?
Now listen to the conversations. Write the words.
1. *Where's the park?*
    The park is {<u>next to</u>} the bank. It's {<u>between</u>} the bank and the supermarket.
2. *Where's the hospital?*
    The hospital is to {<u>the right of</u>} the bookstore. It's in {<u>the middle</u>} of the block.
3. *Excuse me. Where's the department store?*
    The department store is {<u>across from</u>} the shoe store. It's {<u>on the corner</u>} of Second Avenue and Main Street.
4. *Excuse me. Is there a music store around here?*
    The music store is {<u>around the corner</u>} from the library. Turn {<u>left</u>} at the signal.
• Check by having the students read out their answers together.

CONVERSATION GUIDE
• After practicing, students can continue using other places on the map.
Listen.
1. *A: Where's the bank?*
    B: It's between the movie theater and the video shop.
    A: Between the theater and the video shop. Thanks.
    B: You're welcome.
2. *A: Excuse me. How do I get to the video shop?*
    B: Go down this street one block. Turn right at the coffee shop.
    A: Right at the coffee shop?
    B: Yes. It's in the middle of the block.
    A: On the right or the left?
    B: It's on your left.
    A: Thank you.
Practice the conversations.

GROUP RESPONSE

• If students make errors in the responses, try the "finger signal" correction technique explained on page 77.
• Ask each question two times. Allow enough time for all the students to think before gesturing for them to answer.

Look at the map. Answer the questions. Use these words.

1. *Where's the video shop?*
   {It's between the bank and the shoe store.}
2. *Where's the restaurant?*
   {It's next to the school.}
3. *Where's the drug store?*
   {It's across from the hospital.}
4. *Is there a library near here?*
   {It's on the corner of Fifth Street and River Avenue.}
5. *Where's the supermarket?*
   {It's around the corner from the library.}
6. *Is there a bus stop on Sixth Street?*
   {It's in the middle of the block.}

Start at the drug store.

7. *How do I get to the shoe store?*
   {Go to Fifth Street. Turn right. It's on your left.}
8. *How do I get to the school?*
   {Go to the Fifth Street. Turn left. It's across from the supermarket.}

PAIR PRACTICE

• Some students may use "short forms" instead of entire sentences. This is a natural way to give information in English.

UNIT 8: ACTIVE VOCABULARY

(around the) corner	between	block	middle
straight	turn	bank	book store	library
park	restaurant	school	shoe store	music store
video shop	movie theater	supermarket	department store

WARM–UP/EXPANSION ACTIVITIES

• **Where Was It?** Students work in groups of four or five. Each member puts three or four objects (keys, ruler, pen, etc.) on a desk. The objects are mixed and arranged to show different locations (in, on, under, etc.). All students except one close their eyes. That student changes the positions of two objects. Then the others look and try to be the first to say what was moved and where it used to be. (The ruler was in the book. Now it's on the pen.)
• **Eyes-Closed Directions.** Students work in pairs. Scatter a lot of small objects (poker chips work well) around the room. One student in each pair closes his or her eyes. The partner must direct that student to as many chips as possible. The students whose eyes are closed pick them up. The pair that gets the most chips is the winner.

UNIT 9: Present Actions

Note: See pages 75–77 for teaching procedures, strategies, and hints. All activities except the pair practice are on the cassette.

CONVERSATION GUIDE

Listen.

1. *A: Hello.*
      B: Hi, Sara. This is Bob. What are you doing?
   A: Not much. I'm just reading the newspaper and drinking a cup of coffee.
      B: Turn on the TV.
   A: Why?
      B: There's a rock concert on Channel 8. They're playing some great music.
   A: Thanks for telling me.
2. *A: Hello.*
      B: Hi. This is Kim. Is your sister there?
   A: No, she isn't. She's working right now.
      B: How about your brother?
   A: He's at the library. He's studying for a big test.
      B: Oh, OK. I'll call back later.

Practice the conversations.

• This unit practices the present progressive (or present continuous) tense. It is usually used to describe actions that are taking place at the time they are mentioned. Usually, it is used when one speaker cannot see the action (such as on the telephone). It can also be used to identify people (My mother is the woman wearing the blue jacket.) or to call attention to the action (Please be quiet. I'm studying.). The form can also be used for future events (I can't go to the party. I'm working Friday.).

GROUP RESPONSE

• After doing the activity, you may want to have students close their books. Pantomime each action (in a different order than the activity). Students say what they think you're doing.

What are these people doing? Say the answers.

1. *What's he doing?* {He's eating dinner.}
   What's she doing? {She's drinking coffee.}
2. *What are they doing?* {They're cooking.}
3. *What's she doing?* {She's reading a book.}
   What's he doing? {He's listening to music.}
4. *What's she doing?* {She's playing tennis.}
5. *What are they doing?* {They're singing and dancing.}
6. *What's she doing?* {She's talking on the phone.}

FOCUS

• Sentences 6–8 are a new type of activity. Make sure the students understand that they are to write about themselves. Do this by asking Question 6 of a few students. When they answer orally, have them write their own answers in their books.

• Questions 6–8 present a slightly different use of the present progressive tense. Here, students are using it to describe habitual (regularly done) actions rather than those happening at the moment.

Listen. Finish the sentences.

1. *Peter's drinking {tea} and reading a {newspaper}.*
2. *Where are they {going}?*
3. *What {is} he {doing}?*
4. *She's going {shopping}.*
5. *You're not {sleeping}, are you?*

Imagine. What are you doing...? Answer the questions.

6. *It's 7 o'clock in the morning. What are you doing?*
7. *It's 5 o'clock in the afternoon. What are you doing?*
8. *It's 10:30 at night. What are you doing?*

Compare answers with your classmates. Say your answers (6–8). How many other students gave the same answers? Write the numbers.

• If students are reluctant to read out their sentences to compare, have them all stand. They can sit down when they say a sentence.

PAIR PRACTICE

• Note that both A and B have the same picture but different people are labeled.
• Parts 2 and 3 will take on a more game-like atmosphere if students do more than one action at a time or if they do the actions in a way that is difficult to notice.

UNIT 9: ACTIVE VOCABULARY

clap	close	drink	fighting
laugh	play	raise	scratch
sing	sit	sleeping	smile
throw	touch	wave	whistle
talk (on the phone)			

WARM–UP/EXPANSION ACTIVITIES

• **Stick Figures Creativity Test.** Draw 6–8 simple stick figures on the chalkboard. They should be in different positions with the actions unclear. Each student imagines what the people are doing and writes one sentence for each. Then they work in groups of four. They compare answers. Anytime a student wrote an idea that no partner wrote, that person gets a point. If all answers are different, everyone gets a point. The winner is the person with the most points.

• **Human Robots.** Have all students stand. Tell them they will be human robots. Clap your hands at an even rate (about one second between each clap). Every time you clap, they must make a mechanical, robot-like movement with their arms or legs. When you say, "Stop!", they "freeze" in position. They think of some human activity they could be doing if they were in that position. In turns, they pantomime the rest of the action while students nearby guess the actions (You're playing tennis. You're dancing. etc.).

UNIT 10: Problems

Note: See pages 75–77 for teaching procedures, strategies, and hints. All activities except the pair practice are on the cassette.

GROUP RESPONSE

• You may want to stop before the "Say these problems" and the "Say these directions" sections to let students fill in the blanks before they hear the models. Then have them listen, see if they were correct, and repeat.
• "Math" is the short form of "mathematics." It is very common in informal English.

Math Functions. Say these words:
plus, times, minus, divided by, equals (or) is.

Say these problems. Write the verbs.
Four {plus} five equals nine.
Fifteen {divided} by ten is one point five.
Sixty-nine {minus} sixty-eight {equals} one.
Nine {times} eight is seventy-two.

Math Verbs. Say these words:
add, subtract, multiply, divide.

Say these directions. Write the verbs.
{Add} 4 and 5.
{Subtract} 5 from 25.
{Multiply} 8 by 11.
{Divide} 5 by 10.

FOCUS

• For variety, you may want to have the students dictate to each other. To do so, have the first person in each row come to your desk. You read the problem. In turn, they write it and find the answer. Then, they go and tell the problem to the person in the desk behind their own. That person solves the problem, turns and dictates to the next student. At the same time, the first person returns to your desk for the next problem. This continues until all the problems have reached the back of the room.
• Read each problem two times.

Listen. Write the problems. Find the answers. Say them.

1. *6 plus 13 {19}*
2. *125 divided by 5 {25}*
3. *96 minus 13 {83}*
4. *8 times 15 {120}*
5. *Subtract 23 from 58. {35}*
6. *I have 80 dollars... and I'm going to give you 18 dollars... How much do I have now? {80 – 18 = 62}*
7. *The bill is $35... and there are 5 people, so we have to divide it by 5. How much does each person pay? {35 ÷ 5 = 7}*
8. *My rent is $240 a month. I have to pay for January, February, and March... How much do I have to pay? {3 x 240 = 720}*

9. *We need some money for our vacation. I have $850 and you have $675. How much do we have?* {850+675= 1,525}
10. *There were 25 students in the class in September. Three new students came in October. Then 4 students quit the class in November. How many students are there now?* {25 + 3 – 4 = 24}

• Check by having individual students write their answers on the chalkboard or by having the whole class dictate their answers. You or a student writes them on the board.

CONVERSATION GUIDE
Listen.
1. *A: The bill is $27.*
   B: There are four of us, so ...
   A: That's $6.75 each?
   B: Right.
2. *A: How much are these socks?*
   B: They're $4.50 a pair.
   A: I'll take 3 pairs.
   B: OK, that's $13.50.
Practice the conversations.

• You may want to bring in newspaper advertisements which list the prices of many items. After the students have practiced the conversations, they change them to include some of the items in the ads. An alternative is to have students call out items. Write the list on the board. Students then set prices and use the list as they practice.

FOCUS
• Make sure students realize that they will be starting with different numbers. Do this by asking a few what number they wrote after the first step.
• At the end, you might ask who can figure out the trick. How did they all end up with the same number since they started with different numbers? (The trick: They multiplied by two, then divided by the original number. At that point, everyone had "2" as an answer.)
• Read each step two times.
Listen. Follow the instructions. You'll hear each step two times.
Think of a number between 10 and 1,000. Write it.
Multiply by 2.
Now add 5.
Now subtract 8
Now add 3
Now, divide by the first number, the number you thought of.
Multiply by 33.
Subtract 18.
Your answer should be the same number as this page. {48}

PAIR PRACTICE
• Encourage students to check whether they understood by asking "Did you say .... ?"

UNIT 10: ACTIVE VOCABULARY

add	divide(d by)	equals
minus	multiply	plus
subtract	times	bill

WARM–UP/EXPANSION ACTIVITIES
• **Math Race.** Students work in groups of three. One student says a number. The next says another number. The third calls out a math verb (add, subtract, multiply, divide). All three race to solve the problem first. They continue.
• **Pantomime Math.** Students work in groups of four of five. One person thinks of a math problem. He or she pantomimes the numbers using the hand signals they used in the Unit 6 (Large Numbers) Just for Fun. They gesture the function signs (+, x, etc.). The first person to say the answer gets a point and gives the next problem.

REVIEW UNIT: Social Conversation

CONVERSATION GUIDE
Listen.
• Responding
Good news:
1. *A: I got an A on the test.*   *B: That's wonderful.*
2. *A: I got a new job.*   *B: Great!*
3. *A: I won the contest.*   *B: I'm glad to hear that.*
Bad news:
4. *A: My brother is really sick.*   *B: I'm sorry to hear that.*
5. *A: I failed my math test.*   *B: That's too bad.*
6. *A: I lost my wallet.*   *B: That's terrible!*
Neutral (not good or bad):
7. *A: I went to the movies last night.* *B: Really?*
8. *A: I called Lee last night.*   *B: Uh-huh.*

• Giving Advice
9. *A: I have a headache.*   *B: Why don't you take some aspirin?*

10. *A: I'm really tired today.*   *B: You should go to bed earlier.*

• Requesting
11. *A: Could you help me?*   *B: Sure.*
12. *A: Can I borrow your pen?*   *B: Sorry. I'm using it.*
Practice the conversations.

• Like the earlier "social conversation" unit, this lesson has a slightly different purpose than the others in this book. The first page of each introduces standard examples of patterns used for common social interaction. The second page is a review game that covers Units 6–10.
• The procedures for Conversation Guide and Group Response are the same as for the other units (See pages 75–77).
• Some students may be surprised to see "uh-huh" in print. This is a very common expression that lets the other speaker know the person is listening. This "feedback" is an important

part of English. "Uh-huh" is, however, a spoken word. It is rarely used in written English.

• Students sometimes confuse "borrow" (sentence 12) and "lend." "*Borrow*" is what the person who *gets* something does. "*Lend*" is what the person who *gives* it does.

• Because of the social nature of these conversations, you may want to have students move around the classroom. They do each part with a different partner.

GROUP RESPONSE

• Give the students a short time to read the choices before you say each line.

Listen. Choose an answer. Say it and circle the letter.

1. *I lost my wallet.*
    a. {That's too bad.}
2. *I passed the test.*
    b. {That's great!}
3. *I saw a good TV show last night.*
    a. {Uh-huh.}
4. *Could I borrow some money?*
    c. {Sure. Here's five dollars.}
5. *I'm going to visit Canada.*
    b. {That's wonderful.}
6. *Could you help me?*
    c. {Sorry, I'm busy now.}
7. *I didn't pass the math test.*
    a. {That's terrible.}
8. *I feel sick.*
    c. {Why don't you go to the doctor?}
9. *I'm going shopping after school.*
    b. {Really?}
10. *I have a headache.*
    b. {You should take some aspirin.}

THE SMALL TALK GAME

• Students will be familiar with the game if they played the game after Unit 5. Note that the questions are different.

• Be sure they start again after reaching the last square. They should continue until each player has answered at least five questions.

• Tell the students that if they land on a question someone has already answered, they must answer it in a different way. If they land on one of the math problems, they call out a different function (example: "add" instead of "multiply")

• Another option is to make a rule that when a student lands on a question a second time, any partner can ask any question (a different one from the game or one the partner thinks of).

• If dice are available, you may want to use them instead of the "How Many Spaces" box.

• This is a fluency game. Students should be thinking about meaning rather than form. If you hear grammatical errors, note them but don't correct immediately. (See page 77 for more information on corrections.)

UNIT 11: Verb Forms

Note: See pages 75–77 for teaching procedures, strategies, and hints. All activities except the pair practice are on the cassette.

CONVERSATION GUIDE
Listen.
1. *A. What did you do last weekend?*
        B. I visited my parents.
        How about you?
    A. I went shopping. I bought some skis.
        B: When are you going skiing?
    A: Next weekend.
2. *A: Were you in class today?*
        B: No, I was sick.
    A: Are you going to be there tomorrow?
        B: No, I'm going to go to the doctor.
Practice the conversations.

• This unit deals mainly with the simple past and "going to" future. For simplicity, the "will" future is not included. The basic difference between "will" and "going to" is that "going to" is used when the decision to do something is fairly certain. "Will" is used when decisions are less certain, often in the distant future. "Will" is also used at the time a decision is made ("I think I'll watch TV.").

• After they've practiced, have the students change the conversations to be about what they did last weekend and will do soon.

GROUP RESPONSE

• Pause about 2 seconds between each sentence. This will give those students who are able to hear the shorter version a chance to mark their answers. The rest of the students will get the answers after the second sentence.

Listen. Check the times. Say the sentences.
1. *He watched TV.*
        He watched TV {last night}.
2. *They're going to swim.*
        They're going to swim {next Sunday}.
3. *She went dancing.*
        She went dancing {last weekend}.
4. *He visited friends.*
        He visited friends {yesterday}.
5. *She went to Hawaii.*
        She went to Hawaii {last summer}.
6. *They're going to eat dinner at 6 o'clock.*
        They're going to eat dinner at {6 o'clock tonight}.
7. *She studied.*
        She studied {last night}.
8. *They're going to go skiing.*
        They're going to go skiing {next month}.

9. *He wrote some letters.*
    He wrote some letters {yesterday afternoon}.
10. *He's going to go shopping.*
    He's going to go shopping {tomorrow morning}.

PRONUNCIATION
Say each word twice. Pause between them so students can think about the sounds. Pause again before you gesture for them to repeat.
• It's useful to write / d /, / t /, and / ɪd / on the chalkboard. As students say the words, have them point to the correct sound.
The "ed" on a past tense verb makes different sounds.
Listen. Check the sound. Say the words.

1. *called*	{/ d /}
2. *danced*	{/ t /}
3. *played*	{/ d /}
4. *shopped*	{/ t /}
5. *studied*	{/ d /}
6. *visited*	{/ ɪd /}
7. *watched*	{/ t /}

FOCUS
• Like the Focus in Unit 9 (Present Actions), the students are writing about themselves. Make sure they understand this by asking Question 1 to a few students. When they answer, gesture for them to write.
•Read each question two times.
Listen to the questions. Give answers about yourself.
1. *What did you do last night?*
2. *What are you going to do after class today?*
3. *What are you going to do next weekend?*
4. *What did you do last summer?*
5. *Did you eat breakfast today?*
Compare answers with your classmates. Say your answers.
How many other students gave the same answers? Write the numbers.
• If students are reluctant to read out their sentences to compare, have them all stand. They can sit down when they say a sentence.

PAIR PRACTICE
• In talking about their own experiences and plans, students may need more vocabulary. Encourage them to ask in English: How do you say .... in English?

UNIT 11: ACTIVE VOCABULARY

buy – bought	do – did	eat – ate	go – went
ride – rode	see – saw	write – wrote	shop
ski	afternoon	night	weekend
after	cable car	class	interesting
seafood	vacation		

WARM–UP / EXPANSION ACTIVITIES
• **Four Events.** Students work in groups of six to ten. Each takes out a piece of paper and folds it into four sections. On each section, they write one true sentence about something they did in the past. They then tear the sections apart. All sentences are mixed together. One person draws a sentence and reads it aloud. That person guesses who wrote it. If the guess is wrong, anyone else can guess. The person who guesses correctly gets a point. They continue.
• **To Tell the Truth.** Students begin in groups of three. They talk about an interesting experience that one of them has had. They decide on one event. Each group of three joins another group. The original partners tell about the event, each pretending it happened to him or her. The new partners can ask questions. They decide who the story is really about.

UNIT 12: Descriptions

Note: See pages 75–77 for teaching procedures, strategies, and hints. All activities except the pair practice are on the cassette.

PRONUNCIATION
Listen. Say the words.

She's tall.	*She's thin.*	*He's short.*	*He's heavy.*
Hair color brown	black	blond	gray
Eye color brown	blue	green	

She has long hair.	*Her hair is wavy.*
His hair is short.	*He has curly hair.*
She has straight, shoulder-length hair.	*He's bald.*
She's got a pony tail.	*He has a moustache.*
He has a beard.	*She's wearing glasses.*

• After they have done the activity, you may want students to work in pairs. One partner closes the book. The other gestures the words. The first partner says them.
• Other hair colors and styles as well as other description vocabulary are possible. Those included here are the most common. If there are other words you want your students to know, have them write the words here and, perhaps, draw a picture for each.

GROUP RESPONSE
• Read each sentence two times.
Which picture? Listen. Number the pictures (1–9).
1. *This man is bald. He has a moustache.* {G}
2. *He has short, gray hair and a moustache.* {F}
3. *She has curly hair. She is not wearing glasses.* {A}
4. *She has long dark hair. She has a ponytail.* {H}
5. *He's heavy and has glasses.* {C}
6. *He's thin. He has a long beard.* {I}
7. *She's young. She has long, straight black hair.* {B}
8. *She's wearing glasses. She has short, wavy blond hair.* {D}
9. *He's old. He's got gray hair.* {E}

• As a follow-up activity, have students work in pairs. One student thinks of one of the pictures. The partner asks yes/no questions (Is it a woman? Does she have wavy hair? etc.) and tries to guess which picture.

CONVERSATION GUIDE
Listen.
1. A: Do you know Naomi Kato?
    B: I'm not sure. What does she look like?
A: She's got wavy, shoulder-length hair. She has glasses, too.
    B: Is she tall?
A: Yes. Tall and thin.
    B: I think I know her.
2. A: Do you know Jim Wood?
    B: I'm not sure. What does he look like?
A: Well, he has curly blond hair and a moustache.
    B: Is he tall?
A: No. He's short and a little heavy.
    B: Um, I don't think I know him.
Practice the conversations.
• Have students personalize the conversation by describing other people in the class or famous people.

FOCUS
• Students are writing about themselves. When an answer is "no," they should include the correct information in their answer. (example: "No, my hair is black." not "No, it isn't.").
• Read each item two times.
Listen to the questions. Write answers about yourself.
Example: *Question 1.*   *Is your hair brown?*
        You write: *Yes, it is. (or) No, my hair is black.*

1. Is your hair brown?
2. Is your hair long?
3. Is your hair curly?
4. Are you tall or short?
5. What color are your eyes?
6. Does your father have a moustache?
Compare answers with your classmates. Say your answers. How many other students gave the same answers? Write the numbers.
(Student answers will vary).

PAIR PRACTICE
• Note that each character in the picture has a double — someone who looks very similar but is different in one way. This was done to make sure the student would ask several questions about each person.

UNIT 12: ACTIVE VOCABULARY

bald	beard	blond	curly	(wear) glasses
ponytail	short	straight	tall	moustache
thin	heavy	wavy	shoulder-length	

WARM-UP / EXPANSION ACTIVITIES
• **Memory Game.** Students work in pairs. They look at the pictures on the first page of this unit for exactly 2 minutes. Then they close their books. They try to remember as much as possible about what each person looks like. They make notes about each character. They don't need to write complete sentences.
• **Chalkboard Race.** This game requires a large chalkboard if done with a large class. Give a piece of chalk to the first person in each row. Give a short description of a person (He's got long, wavy hair and a beard.). Say the description two times. Then say "Go!" The people with the chalk run to the board and draw a very quick picture including the things you mentioned. The first person to finish and sit down gets a point for his or her row. Then the chalk goes to the second person in the row. Continue.

UNIT 13: Weekend Activities

Note: See pages 75–77 for teaching procedures, strategies, and hints. All activities except the pair practice are on the cassette.

CHOICE
Do you like to do these things? Circle the ones you like. Cross out (X) the ones you don't like. Say the words.
camping, cleaning, cooking, doing homework, hiking, listening to music, playing a musical instrument, reading, riding a bicycle, skiing, studying, swimming, taking tests, using a computer

• Check their responses by drawing a circle on one end of the chalkboard and an X on the other. As they say the words, they point at the circle for those activities they like and the X for those they dislike.

FOCUS: "ing" and "to"
• Make sure students understand that they can check both "verb+ing" and "to + verb" in some cases. Do this by reading the first two sentences. Then have the students repeat what you said. Demonstrate checking both in your book.
• Some verbs go with another verb+ING. *I enjoy swimming.*
Other verbs take to + verb. *I want to ski this winter.*
Some verbs use either verb+ING or to + verb. *I love watching movies. / I love to watch movies.*
Listen. Which do these verbs take? Check the forms you hear.
Example: *A: like*
        B: I like skiing.
        I like to ski.

1. *I like to eat Chinese food. He likes eating it, too.*
    {"ing" and "to"}
2. *I enjoy swimming. She enjoys swimming, too.* BOTH {ing}
3. *She dislikes cleaning her room. He dislikes cleaning, too.*
    BOTH {ing}
4. *I want to ski this winter. She wants to ski, too.* BOTH {to}
5. *She learned to use a a computer last year. He learned to
    use one, too.* BOTH {to}
6. *He hopes to visit Australia. She hopes to visit, too.* BOTH {to}
7. *She feels like going to a movie. He feels like going, too.*
    BOTH {ing}
8. *I hate taking tests. Do you hate to take them, too?*
    {"ing" and "to"}
Check your answers.

CONVERSATION GUIDE
Listen.
1. A: *What are you going to do this weekend?*
   B: *I want to go camping. I really love hiking in the woods.*
   A: *Yeah, I like to hike, too.*
   B: *What are you going to do?*
   A: *Nothing special. I hope to see a movie.*
   B: *That sounds like fun.*
2. A: *Are you doing anything special this weekend?*
   B: *Yeah. I'm taking a cooking class. I'm learning to make
      Indian food.*
   A: *That sounds interesting.*
   B: *It is. I really enjoy cooking.*
   A: *Not me. I hate cooking. But I like eating.*
Practice the conversations.

• After they have practiced, have them change the
conversa-tion by using the activities on the previous page as
well as things they did last weekend or are planning for the
near future.

FOCUS
• Make sure students understand they are writing about
themselves.
• Read each item two times.
Listen. Write the answers about yourself. Don't write the questions.
Example: Question 1.   Do you like to ski?
*   You write: Yes, I like to ski.*
*   No, I don't like to ski.*

1. *Do you like to ski?*
2. *Do you love swimming?*
3. *Do you hope to go to the beach?*
4. *Do you enjoy reading?*
5. *Do you feel like going to a movie?*
6. *Do you hate cleaning?*
7. *Do you want to speak English better?*

• Student answers will vary. You may wish to check by
having students raise their hands or by doing a group
response. Have all those who answered "yes" say their
sentence first. Then those who answered "no" say theirs.

PAIR PRACTICE
• If your students are fairly good at speaking, encourage them
to say at least one extra sentence about the information in
Step 2 (Example: I enjoy shopping for clothes. My favorite
store is .... [or] I like buying colorful clothes).

UNIT 13: ACTIVE VOCABULARY

dislike	enjoy	feel	like	hate	hope
learned	like	want	play a musical instrument		
clean	take a test	use a computer	jazz		
rock	classical music	poetry	homework		

WARM–UP /EXPANSION ACTIVITIES
• **That's a Lie.** Students each write four sentences about themselves. Each sentence must contain one of the words from the
Focus activity on the first page of this unit. Three sentences
are true. One is a "lie." Students then circulate, working in
pairs. They read their sentences to a partner. The partner
decides which is untrue and changes it to the negative (I don't
think you enjoy rugby.). After the correct guess, they change
partners and continue.

UNIT 14: Frequency

*Note: See pages 75–77 for teaching procedures, strategies, and
hints. All activities except the pair practice are on the cassette.*

FOCUS
• Between sentences, you may need to pause or stop the tape
and gesture for students to ask for the spelling. Gesture by
pointing to them, then pointing to the "Hint Box."
Listen to the sentences. Ask how to spell the words. Say the sentences.
I {always} eat breakfast. // A-L-W-A-Y-S.
I {usually} eat rice for supper. // U-S-U-A-L-L-Y
I {sometimes} eat lunch at 12:30. // S-O-M-E-T-I-M-E-S
I {hardly ever} eat steak. // H-A-R-D-L-Y E-V-E-R
I {never} drink coffee at night. // N-E-V-E-R

• This unit practices adverbs of frequency. Note that except
for "always" and "never" the meanings are relative. In particular, "sometimes" can include things that are done quite often
as well as those that are not.
• Some students will be more familiar with "rarely" and
"seldom" than with "hardly ever." "Hardly ever" has the same
meaning and is more common in spoken English.

CONVERSATION GUIDE

• You may want to vary the practice by writing some of the activities from the next three pages on the board. Students modify the conversation, asking about the activities.

Listen.

1. *A: Do you like reading?*
   B: Yes. I always read before I go to bed.
   A: Not me. I usually watch TV.
   B: What do you watch?
   A: Sometimes movies. Sometimes the news.
2. *A: How often do you listen to music?*
   B: Every day. I usually listen to jazz.
   A: I hardly ever do. I listen to rock.

Practice the conversations.

GROUP RESPONSE

• You can vary the activity by giving real answers about yourself rather than using the tape. Instead of asking about "David", the students will ask you: "How often do you wake up before 6:30? How often do you eat breakfast before 8?", etc.

Ask the questions. Listen for the answers. Say the sentences.

Use: always, usually, sometimes, hardly ever, never.
Example:
Ask: *How often does David wake up before 6:30?*
Listen *to the answer: Every day.*
Say: *He **always** wakes up before 6:30.*

1. Ask:
   Every day.
   Say: He {always} eats breakfast before 8:00.
2. Ask:
   Three or four nights a week.
   Say: He {sometimes} listens to music at night.
3. Ask:
   Not at all. He doesn't like it.
   Say: He {never} watches professional wrestling.
4. Ask:
   One or two days a month.
   Say: He {hardly ever} works more than 10 hours a day.
5. Ask:
   Five or six nights a week.
   Say: He {usually} reads at night.

FOCUS

• Make sure students understand they are writing about themselves.
• The short form (I usually do.) is more natural than reformulating the question to include the answer (How often do you watch TV after work or school? I usually watch TV after work.).

Listen to the questions. Answer about yourself.

1. *How often do you watch TV after work or school?*
2. *How often do you sleep more than eight hours?*
3. *How often do you eat seafood for dinner?*
4. *How often do you go to movies on Saturday or Sunday?*
5. *How often do you eat fruit for breakfast?*

• Correct by asking the questions again and having students raise their hands to show if they always, usually, etc. do the activities.

PAIR PRACTICE

• You may want to direct one pair through the first two steps of the activity to make sure students understand what to do.
• The students don't need to write down all of the extra information. They may want to take short notes (e.g., "about two times a year" might be reduced to "2 x yr").
• Some of the extra information is in the form of sentence fragments (incomplete sentences) rather than full sentences. This is natural, especially in spoken English.

UNIT 14: ACTIVE VOCABULARY

always	usually	sometimes	hardly ever
never	breakfast	lunch	dinner
eat	movies	news	study
wake up	favorite	broken	

WARM–UP/EXPANSION ACTIVITIES

• **Class Poll.** Have each student decide on a frequency question that is interesting. It can be one from the Pair Practice, the Focus, the Group Response or one the student thinks of. They write their questions on a piece of paper. Then they write the frequency adverbs (always, usually, etc.). Students stand and circulate. They ask their questions of at least 15 other students. They write the answers next to the adverbs. At the end, they can report to the entire class the results of the poll.

• **My Favorite Teacher.** List the five adverbs on the board. Students work in pairs. Each thinks of the best teacher they have ever had. What did the teacher always do? What did the teacher do sometimes? They think of one sentence for each word. They tell their partner. The partner responds by saying if his or her favorite teacher did the thing with the same frequency. Variation: Instead of a favorite teacher, do the activity on one of the following topics:

My best friend.
Foods I like and don't like.
A pet.
My own bad habits.
Someone I really don't like (Don't say names!)

UNIT 15: Processes

Note: See pages 75–77 for teaching procedures, strategies, and hints. All activities except the pair practice are on the cassette.

GROUP RESPONSE
• This unit practices the imperative, a common form for giving orders and directions. Imperatives usually don't have subjects unless it is necessary to show who is being told to do something (Bill, stand up.). "You" at the beginning of an imperative sentence often shows anger (You sit down!).
• Because the students are doing physical actions, you may want to have them stand during this activity.
• After they've done the activity, an enjoyable review is to have them work in groups of 4 or 5. One person says a command. The others try to be the first to do the action. The winner gives the next command.

Do the actions. Say the words.

Point to the door	Touch your book	Hold a pen	Raise your hand	Clap your hands
Write A-B-C	Draw a house	Close your book	Open your book	Stand up
Sit down	Push	Pull	Pour	Fill

FOCUS
Note: Students ask you the questions on the left.
• Read each answer two times.
• Since the students already know how to make tea, you may want to have them fill in the blanks before they listen. Then they listen and check to see if they were correct.

Ask the questions. Write the missing words.
1. First, {fill} the kettle.
2. {Put it} on the {stove}.
3. {Wait} until the {water} boils.
4. {Put} the tea bag {in the cup}.
5. {Pour} the water {into the cup}.

CONVERSATION GUIDE
• Have students act out the process as they practice. Then have them change the conversation to be about other machines such as a video player, a CD player, a computer, or any others they are familiar with.

Listen.
A: *Excuse me. How does this microwave oven work?*
  B: *It's easy. First, put the food in.*
A: *OK.*
  B: *Now, set the temperature control.*
A: *How do I do that?*
  B: *Just push this button.*
A: *I see. What's next?*
  B: *Set the timer.*
A: *OK.*
  B: *Last, press the start button.*
A: *That's all?*
  B: *Right. When the bell rings, your food is ready.*
A: *Thanks.*
Practice the conversation.

PRONUNCIATION
• You may want to have the students draw the shapes in the air as they repeat the words. For further practice, you draw them quickly in the air as the students call out the words.
Say these words.
square   rectangle   triangle   circle   line

FOCUS: Following Directions
• Don't be overly concerned about the size of the figures they draw. The important thing in this lesson is the vocabulary and the forms used.
• Read each item two times.

Listen. Draw the picture.
1. *Draw a large square.*
2. *Draw a rectangle under the square.*
3. *Draw a circle on the square.*
4. *Put a triangle in the square.*
5. *Put a line over the circle.*
6. *Write your name to the left of the square.*

• Step 6 will make sure the students drew the picture correctly. The students' drawings will look similar to the following:

GROUP RESPONSE
• Prompt the students to tell you how to draw the picture. Draw it exactly as they describe it, even if there are mistakes in meaning. This will require them to go back and correct the mistakes. If there are mistakes in grammar, repeat the instruction correctly (example: Students: "Draw square." Teacher: "Draw a square? OK."

PAIR PRACTICE
• If you want the students to go on and have their partners draw pictures more complex than the ones in Steps 1 and 2, teach the the following vocabulary: horizontal (—), vertical (|), diagonal (/ , \ ).

UNIT 15: ACTIVE VOCABULARY

boil	draw	fill	hold
point	pour	pull	push
set	sit down	stand up	finally
first	next	then	circle
line	rectangle	square	triangle
control	timer	temperature	

WARM–UP/EXPANSION ACTIVITIES

• **Five Times Fast.** Students work in pairs. Each pair thinks of a machine they know how to use or a process they can do. They write a dialogue similar to those in the conversation guide. They then practice reading the dialogue five times in a row as fast as they can. Variation: Have pairs exchange dialogues. They check the new conversation, correcting errors when possible. They then try to read the conversation five times as quickly as they can.

• **Simon Says.** Students work in groups of four or five. One person is Simon (the leader). That person gives a series of commands using the verbs from this unit. Each command starts with the words "Simon says...". (Simon says touch your desk. Simon says stand up. etc.) The other students do the actions. When the leader say a command without saying "Simon says..." (Sit down!) any student who does the action is out. That person becomes the next leader.

REVIEW UNIT: Social Conversation

• Like the earlier "social conversation" units, this lesson has a slightly different purpose than the others in this book. The first page of each introduces standard examples of patterns used for common social interaction. The second page is a review game that covers Units 11–15.
• The procedures for Conversation Guide and Group Response are the same as for the other units (See pages 75–77).

CONVERSATION GUIDE

• Because of the social nature of these conversations, you may want to have students move around the classroom. They do each part with a different partner.
• Note the phrase "I'd better..." in sentence 6. "...had better..." is used for saying what the speaker needs to do or for giving advice (You had better see a doctor). It is fairly strong and is not usually used for making suggestions. For suggesting, "How about..." is more appropriate.

Listen.

• Offering
1. *A: Would you like a cup of coffee?* B: *Yes, please.*
   A: Do you want cream and sugar? B: *No thanks. Just black.*

2. *A: How about something to eat?* B: *No thanks. I'm not hungry.*

• Apologizing
3. *A: What happened?* B: *I'm sorry I'm late. I missed the bus.*

4. *A: Oh, no! I'm really sorry.* B: *That's OK. Don't worry.*

   A: Let me clean it up.

• Ending a Conversation
5. *A: Well, I need to get to class.* B: *Yeah. See you tomorrow.*

6. *A: It's getting late. I'd better be going.* B: *Me, too. Goodbye.*

Practice the conversations.

GROUP RESPONSE

• Give the students a short time to read the choices before you say each line.

Listen. Choose an answer. Say it and circle the letter.

1. *Would you like something to drink?* b. {Yes. Cola, please.}
2. *Oh, I'm really sorry.* c. {That's OK. Don't worry about it.}
3. *Do you want some help?* b. {No, thanks.}
4. *It's getting late. I'd better be going.* a. {Yeah. See you tomorrow.}
5. *How about some ice cream? Do you want chocolate or vanilla?* c. {Vanilla, please.}
6. *Oh, I need to catch the bus.* b. {Goodbye.}
7. *Would you like something to eat?* c. {No, thanks. I'm not hungry.}
8. *I'm sorry I'm late. I missed my train.* a. {That's OK.}

THE SMALL TALK GAME

• Students will be familiar with the game if they played after Unit 5 or Unit 10. Note that the questions are different.
• Be sure they start again after reaching the last square. They should continue until each player has answered at least six questions.
• Tell the students that if they land on a question someone has already answered, they must answer it in a different way.
• Another option: make a rule that when a student lands on a question a second time, any partner can ask any question (a different one from the game or one the partner thinks of).
• If dice are available, you may want to use them instead of the "How Many Spaces" box.
• This is a fluency game. Students should be thinking about meaning rather than form. If you hear grammatical errors, note them but don't correct immediately. (See page 78 for more information on corrections.)